JANET K. RUFFING, R.S.M.

SPIRITUAL DIRECTION

Beyond the Beginnings

PAULIST PRESS
New York / Mahwah, N.J.

Scripture quotations are taken from the Revised Standard Version Common Bible, copyright 1973, Division of Christian Education of the National Council of the Churches of Christ in the USA.

The Publisher acknowledges *Presence: The Journal of Spiritual Directors International* (www.sdiworld.org) for portions of chapter 4 that first appeared in the January 1995 issue in an article by the author entitled: "Encountering Love Mysticism."

The Publisher gratefully acknowledges use of the following: Excerpts from *Telling Secrets* by Frederick Buechner, copyright 1991 by Frederick Buechner. Reprinted by permission of HarperCollins Publishers, Inc. Excerpts from *Beguine Spirituality*, edited and introduced by Fiona Bowie and translated by Oliver Davies, copyright 1990, by Fiona Bowie and Oliver Davies. Reprinted by permission. Excerpts from *Manifestations of Grace* by Elizabeth Dreyer, copyright 1990. Reprinted by permission of Liturgical Press. Excerpts from *The Collected Works of St. Teresa of Avila* (Volume One), translated by Kieran Kavanaugh and Otilio Rodriguez, copyright 1976 by the Washington Province of Discalced Carmelites/ICS Publications; 2131 Lincoln Road, N.E.; Washington, D.C. 20002 USA. Excerpts from *John of the Cross: Selected Writings*, translated by Kieran Kavanaugh, copyright 1987 by the Washington Province of Discalced Carmelites Friars, Inc. Reprinted by permission of Paulist Press. Excerpts from *Hadewijch: The Complete Works*, translated by Mother Columba Hart, copyright 1980 by the Missionary Society of Saint Paul the Apostle in the State of New York. Reprinted by permission of Paulist Press. Excerpts from *The Spiritual Exercises of Saint Ignatius*, translated by Louis J. Puhl, copyright 1951. Reprinted by permission of Loyola Press. Excerpt from "Burnt Norton" in *The Complete Poems and Plays, 1909–1950*, copyright 1930 and renewed 1958 by T. S. Eliot. Reprinted by permission of Harcourt Brace & Company and Faber and Faber, Ltd.

Cover design by Cynthia Dunne

Ruffing, Janet, 1945-
Spiritual direction : beyond the beginnings / Janet K. Ruffing.
p. cm.
Includes bibliographical references.
ISBN 0-8091-3958-8 (alk. paper)
1. Spiritual direction. I. Title.
BX 2350.7.R83 2000
253.5′3—dc21
00-028558

Published by Paulist Press
997 Macarthur Boulevard
Mahwah, New Jersey 07430

www.paulistpress.com

Printed and bound in the
United States of America

Table of Contents

Introduction
        Beyond the Beginnings 1

Chapter 1
        Praying for What We Want:
        Sorting Out Our Desires 9

Chapter 2
        Endlessly Inventive Evasion:
        Resistance in Spiritual Direction 33

Chapter 3
        "Panning for Gold":
        Attending to Theological Themes
        in Spiritual Direction 57

Chapter 4
        Searching for the Beloved:
        Love Mysticism in Spiritual Direction 95

Chapter 5
        Mutuality with God:
        "Where Beloved and Loved One Shall
        Wholly Flow Through Each Other" 125

Chapter 6
        The "As If" Relationship:
        Transference and Countertransference
        in Spiritual Direction 155

Epilogue 181

Acknowledgments

This volume on spiritual direction is the fruit of more than twenty years of engaging in this ministry. I am grateful to both my directees and interviewees from my research sample who have so generously shared their lives with me and given me permission to use their narratives in teaching and in writing. My spiritual direction students in the Graduate School of Religion and Religious Education at Fordham since 1986 have compelled me to articulate many of the themes in this book in the process of helping them discern their own calls to become spiritual directors. My psychologist colleagues, Dr. Fredrica Halligan, Dr. Mary Byrne, and Dr. Beverly Musgrave, who have worked with me and my cosupervisors, Margaret Ellen Burke, S.C., and Katherine King, F.S.P., in the practicum experience as consultants and supervisors, have deepened my insights about some of the psychological aspects of both spiritual direction and supervision.

The three-day Ignatian Spirituality Institute in August, 1995, sponsored by the Oregon province of the Society of Jesus, required me to draft initial versions of four chapters of this volume so that responders could expand and develop my themes. I am grateful to Stacey Cates-Carney, Andy Dufner, S.J., L. Patrick Carroll, and Cindy Rose, who responded to my initial presentations, and to the entire group of spiritual directors whose questions and responses refined my thinking. Joyceann Hagan, coordinator of the entire program, graciously provided videotapes of these sessions so I could recapture some of those spontaneous interchanges and incorporate them into the text.

Among the other chapters of this volume, "Panning for Gold" and "Love Mysticism in Spiritual Direction" were initially presented as workshops to spiritual directors or supervisors at national symposia or conferences sponsored by the

Spiritual Directors International in Atchison, Kansas, in 1994, and "Transference and Countertransference" in Burlingame, California, in 1998. *Presence: The Journal of Spiritual Directors International* originally published "Encountering Love Mysticism: Issues in Supervision" in its inaugural issue, January, 1995, and has given me permission for this revised form of the material.

A public lecture cosponsored by the Aquinas Institute and the St. Louis Region of Spiritual Directors International gave me the occasion to present the chapter on mutuality with God to a fresh audience while I was working on this manuscript.

The final manuscript was written in St. Louis while I was coministering in the Mercy Collaborative Novitiate. I owe special thanks to each of the women in the novitiate community who provided support for my writing despite the demands of the novitiate process, and especially to Celeste Marie Nuttman, R.S.M., my friend and cominister in the novitiate. The St. Louis Regional Community of the Sisters of Mercy offered beautiful grounds and living space at Mercy Center, and the sisters there were good companions as I wrote and lived among them.

Fordham University's faculty fellowship for 1998–99 provided above all time as well as the necessary financial support not only for this book but for several other writing projects as well. And finally, Kathleen Walsh, my editor at Paulist, greatly improved the text through her perceptive reading and questions as well as her careful attention to detail.

To My Parents,
George (1914–2000) and Dorothy Ruffing,
who continue to inspire me despite the challenges of their latter years

BEYOND THE BEGINNINGS

The ministry of spiritual direction within the churches continues to enjoy a renaissance at the beginning of the twenty-first century. This resurgence of interest in the practice of spiritual direction and its unique contemporary development has resulted in a number of trends. Spiritual direction training programs continue to flourish—as evidenced by more than three hundred such programs in pastoral or academic settings in the United States. From an ascetical discipline primarily practiced by men and women in Roman Catholic religious orders since the sixteenth century, spiritual direction is now sought by women and men in every lifestyle within the churches. Likewise, those charismatically gifted by God's Spirit with a call to offer spiritual direction to others also include men and women in every lifestyle and across the Christian denominations. The complexities of contemporary life, with its peculiar challenges to faith, and the breadth of choices Christians face daily lead many to seek individual guidance and support in their ongoing life of intimacy with God and discernment about their responses to this relationship in the daily concerns of life and discipleship.

A wide variety of books that literally introduce directors and directees to the practice of spiritual direction in its beginning stages already exists. There are excellent treatments of the history of spiritual direction, of discernment, of spiritual direction and its distinction from therapy or counseling, of spiritual direction and developmental psychology, and of spiritual direction for particular populations such as gays and lesbians, women, men, and so forth. *Spiritual Direction: Beyond the Beginnings* represents a particular contribution to the practice of spiritual direction for both spiritual directors and directees (persons who seek the assistance of another in relationship to their own spiritual direction) who have, indeed, progressed "beyond the beginnings" of the initial phases of spiritual direction and the beginnings of an intentional spiritual life.

In my first book on spiritual direction, *Uncovering Stories of Faith: Narrative and Spiritual Direction*, I explored spiritual direction as a hermeneutical process of Christian identity formation through the process of oral autobiography. This basic narrative process remains fundamental to spiritual direction and is assumed in this volume. When I researched and wrote that book fifteen years ago, I was still at the beginning of my practice of this ministry as a spiritual director and supervisor. I offer these reflections from my current vantage point of continuously practicing spiritual direction and supervising intern spiritual directors.

The following reflections focus on advanced themes, issues, and dynamics that occur in directees' spiritual lives and in the process of spiritual direction itself, and that require continuous and careful attention on the part of spiritual directors. There has been, in the past, a noticeable lack of written material on the subject of mature spiritual development and the experience and issues of directees who have remained in spiritual direction for more than five years after a spiritual awakening. *Spiritual Direction: Beyond the Beginnings* addresses this lacuna in the literature and represents some of my most significant learning as a spiritual director and supervisor.

Introduction

All six chapters were originally developed and tested in workshops for spiritual directors, either at the national meeting of Spiritual Directors International and its Symposium for Trainers or at the Ignatian Spirituality Institute, sponsored by the Northwest Province of Jesuits. These chapters are informed by my research as a scholar in the academic discipline of spirituality and, hopefully, will prove accessible to ordinary readers who have themselves progressed beyond the beginnings and who may benefit personally and ministerially from these reflections.

In addition to focusing "beyond the beginnings" of spiritual life and spiritual direction, I also attempt to remain attentive to the particular experience and needs of women, who presently constitute the majority of spiritual directors and directees, according to the recorded membership of Spiritual Directors International. Other ongoing research on the path to God through sense, symbol, and relationship, which I am conducting, has afforded me rich accounts of interviewees' experiences, along with their full permission to use them in my writings.

This volume proceeds through a series of topics that I approach both theoretically (in many cases) and practically. The more general reader who is interested in spiritual direction from the perspective of a directee can easily skip over the parts that may be of greater benefit and interest to spiritual directors. Since there is a self-guiding element in the spiritual life that develops from reading and reflection, some of these sections may, in fact, illumine experiences for particular directees.

I offer spiritual directors an opportunity to reflect on their experience both as directors and as directees and raise a variety of concerns in each chapter "beyond the beginnings." Some directors may not yet have directees who present some of the issues I discuss. Others may discover some new understandings to support their practice of accompaniment. Both beginning and advanced spiritual directors have responded positively to this material as I developed it, and have helped test my insights.

With this practical end in mind, each chapter elucidates a particular theme through theory, illustrative case material, verbatims, or examples, and each provides a set of questions for further reflection. The endnotes for each chapter not only account for my sources but also make available further reading on each topic.

Before describing the sequence of content in the volume, I want to discuss the way I refer to the *Spiritual Exercises* of St. Ignatius in the chapters that follow. A large number of Roman Catholic spiritual directors have been trained as spiritual directors through the process of making the Ignatian Exercises, first as retreatants (often several times), and were subsequently taught how to direct the retreat process based on the *Exercises*. The latter is a specialized form of spiritual direction that includes all of the ordinary dynamics of spiritual direction as well as the specific content and focus of the structured processes and series of contemplations comprising this retreat, either in its thirty-week format, thirty-day format, or six-to-eight-day format. Many directors who may not have had the opportunity to study spiritual traditions within Christianity beyond the Ignatian approach may be unaccustomed to viewing the core themes in the *Exercises* through other lenses of interpretation. In this volume, I address some of the central themes of the *Exercises* that every spiritual director, regardless of background or denomination, will eventually encounter in some way, whether in ongoing spiritual direction or in the retreat direction process. It is in this context that I identify and associate a given theme with the *Exercises*.

My framework, however, while including a thorough grasp of the dynamics of this particular and powerful spiritual tool, is more expansive than the Ignatian point of view alone. Thus, my treatment includes material from the women's spiritual tradition and reflection on its core themes and dynamics without focusing particularly on retreat processes or Ignatian terminology alone. Other chapters began with a theme I was discovering in my own experience as a spiritual director and supervisor. In order to show the relevance to this material for directors working with the *Exercises*, I indicate how it might emerge in relationship to the *Spiritual Exercises* but do not make this a major focus of the discussion.

Spiritual directors who are unfamiliar with the *Spiritual Exercises* should be able to reflect on their experience of these themes and dynamics from their own contexts without reference to the work itself. The Exercises themselves were simply Ignatius's way of organizing and using the major spiritual practices of his own day. Thus, he participated in a tradition from which he drew and to which he contributed. In this volume, I tend to draw on the wider tradition and supplement an Ignatian point of view with other perspectives and sources, including contemporary ones.

The volume begins with a treatment of desire in prayer and in the spiritual life. This theme goes back to Augustine and is related to a spiritual path of intensifying and expressing desire, even passionate desire, as a way of focusing energy in the quest for God. Psychology and psychoanalytic theory has taught us that we are not always conscious of our real desires or aware of conflicts among our desires. Ignatius employs a practice of focusing every meditation and contemplation through a particular desire. When we pray, we express what we want. This chapter explores the process of sorting out our desires and the progressive pattern of spiritual growth that occurs when we engage and pray with our honest and authentic desires. Often in entertaining and engaging our desires we grow in self-knowledge about them, and we open ourselves to God's influence and fulfillment of those desires.

Chapter 2 describes the complex experience of resistance in spiritual direction. It helps directors better understand the particular forms resistance—to prayer, to spiritual experience, to a content or theme, or even to the spiritual director—may take within the process of spiritual direction. Since resistance, or avoidance of a content or even the implication of religious experience, is by definition unconscious, spiritual directors need to understand and expect resistance to emerge "beyond the beginnings" of the spiritual life especially and to learn how they might respond in helpful ways to their directees' difficulties with avoidance.

Chapter 3 is both subtler and more technical. Since clergy became responsible for spiritual direction from the sixteenth century to the present, a theological approach to the ministry was central. In this earlier context directors were charged with judging the doctrinal orthodoxy of their directees' religious experiences and reflections. In the contemporary situation, many spiritual directors may not be theologically trained if they have not pursued an academic degree in pastoral ministry or theology. As a result, they may tend not to recognize their own operative theologies or the theological themes emerging from their directees' experiences. This chapter briefly offers a theological basis for the process of spiritual direction in terms of a theology of grace and challenges spiritual directors to work with theological themes that spontaneously emerge from their directees' narratives. Rather than evaluating and judging directees' emerging theological reflection, I recommend that directors help directees recognize their personal appropriation of the mysteries of Christian faith as a logical development of their deepening spiritual lives. The focus is more on what and how God is revealing God's self to the directee than on the exact personal theological expression of the directee.

Chapter 4 explores a particular strand of religious experience, sometimes called "love mysticism," in spiritual direction. When the focus on desire (introduced in chapter 1) becomes central in directees' spiritual lives—expressly as passion for God with erotic overtones—many directees and their directors develop specific kinds of resistance to the experience either through fear or ignorance of this tradition. On the whole, love mysticism seems to be more characteristic of women than men. In this chapter I describe how directors might support their directees' unfolding mystical experience, another manifestation of the spiritual life "beyond the beginnings."

Chapter 5 represents an even fuller development of love mysticism when we or our directees begin to discover mutuality with God, a genuine partnering with God made possible as a result of transforming grace. Because this is a neglected theme in the spiritual tradition—and one that many of us were taught was not even likely or possible—there is a more extensive treatment of the issue. Many directors and directees easily become confused when encountering this phenomenon because it confounds conventional expectations. This provides another example "beyond the beginnings" in which a more accurate experiential vision of this potential development can enable directors to better support their directees in this mature unfolding of their spiritual development.

Finally, in chapter 6 I address the experience of transference and countertransference in spiritual direction. This chapter may be of greatest interest and assistance to directors who are responsible, as pastoral ministers, for maintaining the sacred trust of their directees. Part of this responsibility requires awareness of and management of transference and countertransference so that directees are not harmed in their spiritual development by the anxiety or fear they may evoke in their directors. The ability to reflect on the experience of spiritual direction at this level is the final experience "beyond the beginnings," which I treat in this volume. Transference, the unconscious projections of our directees, takes time to develop. Attention to transference and awareness of the particular forms it may take in the spiritual direction process, especially when directors work with particular directees for a number of years, are ethical responsibilities that require some psychological sophistication from the director.

I hope these reflections on themes and experiences of spiritual direction, which typically occur "beyond the beginnings" of accompanying directees in spiritual direction, will stimulate thought and reflection of both directors and directees and ultimately contribute to more skillful spiritual direction.

Chapter 1

PRAYING FOR WHAT WE WANT: SORTING OUT OUR DESIRES

What do we really want? Human and divine desiring is a core feature of the spiritual life. Our desires energize the spiritual quest and lead us to God. Of even greater surprise is the possibility that God longs for us as much as we do for God. Desire is so ubiquitous in human experience that spiritual directors are likely to spend a considerable amount of time exploring and even focusing directees' desires. Different streams of the Christian spiritual tradition offer guidance and suggest a variety of approaches. Directors need to develop great skill in recognizing and responding to their directees' desire for God and in helping directees uncover illusory desires.

Mechthild of Magdeburg amazingly describes both the "Soul's" desiring and God's desiring. She says from our side this is how the Soul speaks to God:

> God, you are my lover,
> My longing,
> My flowing stream,
> My sun,
> And I am your reflection.

From God's side, this is how God answers the Soul:

> It is my nature that makes me love you often,
> For I am love itself.
> It is my longing that makes me love you intensely,
> For I yearn to be loved from the heart.
> It is my eternity that makes me love you long,
> For I have no end.[1]

In the beginning of the spiritual life, we feel as if all the desiring is on our side. Mechtild's mystical insight suggests otherwise. She boldly asserts that God's longing evokes and fuels our own. That God's own self initiates these longings.

Desire in the Exercises

Spiritual directors trained to give the Spiritual Exercises of St. Ignatius encounter one version of this theme in the particular way Ignatius repeatedly advises the retreatant to "ask God our Lord for what I want and desire" in the second prelude for each meditation.[2] As the retreat proceeds Ignatius tells the retreatant exactly what to desire. Ignatius specifies a particular sequence of desiring, which structures a process of conversion and increasing affective intimacy with "Christ, our Lord."

This central focus on ten specific desires, which correspond to the content of each cycle of contemplation, is one of the most exquisite strengths of the process of the Exercises. At the same time, it can be one of the most problematic dynamics in the retreat.

The specification of desire is a powerful technique that unifies the desires of the retreatant toward a particular grace and leads to a progressive intimate relationship and identification with Jesus. It is problematic, however, because our desires are not always accessible to us. Directees, retreatants, and spiritual directors do not necessarily know what they most authentically want. It takes great skill and sensitivity on the part of spiritual directors to assist their directees in discovering their desires and interpreting them correctly so that they can uncover God's desires for them in the depths of their own desiring.

Spiritual directors shaped by their own experience of the Ignatian Exercises, through which they have personally experienced their own authentic desiring, typically ask retreatants or directees what their current desire is. For what are directees praying? What do they want? How can and ought they pray for what they want?

Desire in Christian Tradition

Mechthild and Ignatius, along with Augustine, Bernard, and countless others in the Christian mystical tradition, assume that God's yearning for us precedes and arouses our yearning for God. This is a profound spiritual reality. Our desiring already originates in God's desiring us. Too often we and our directees approach prayer as if we want something and God most likely wants something else. These mystics go deeper. They strongly assert that our desires, our wants, our longings, our outward and inward searching—when uncovered, expressed, and recognized—all lead to the Divine Beloved at the core. As Augustine so tellingly phrased it in the *Confessions*, "Our Hearts are restless until they rest in you, O God." God is our hearts' desiring. Our insatiable desires lead us right into the Holy Mystery itself, which is their origin and goal.

I propose that all our desires ultimately lead us to God. We often don't recognize the deeper things for which we long because it is not a *thing* we really want but a deeper relationship with God. We long for the Holy Mystery itself to possess us.

This approach to God through love and longing is in marked contrast to the Buddhist tradition, which frequently influences many of us and our directees. According to Buddhism's four noble truths, the cause of all human suffering is desire and attachment. Buddhist meditators actually "vow to extinguish desire." The Buddhists suggest that it is our very attachment to our wants, our willing, and our cravings that creates suffering. Thus, major spiritual traditions offer two radically different approaches—one through desire and one through extinguishing desire.

Why do Buddhists reject desire? One reason is that wanting and desiring tend to propel us into the future. It can easily take us out of the present, where God or Ultimate Reality is (and where we are too) into possibly illusory, unrealizable fantasy. There is some element of desire that can never be satisfied. That frustration leads some into an addictive form of craving that enslaves—the cause of suffering according to the Buddha. For others, the immediate frustration develops into a form of hope rather than craving. The Buddha's teaching from another point of view is actually quite similar to the Christian mystic. The Buddha recognized a distorted, illusory quality to desires and taught his disciples simply to bracket or ignore them. In that process, absolute reality became available. Christian mystics of the affective type recommend intensifying desire to the point of transparency. Both approaches take the meditator or pray-er beyond conventional and superficial wants.

Discovering What We Really Want

I am convinced that many Christians never entertain their desires long enough to know what they really want. If we habitually suppress our wants, we may never discover the true core of our longing that could lead us more deeply into God. It takes courage to allow our desires to become conscious. When they do, we become responsible for either participating in their fulfillment—moving toward that which we desire—or participating in their frustration—failing to act on our desire.

Many of us have been conditioned to expect our desires to be frustrated anyway. We are sure we are never going to get what we want. There are a lot of "spoilers" in Christian tradition. There exists a very strong misperception that what we really want will surely be at odds with God's will. Our wills are usually equated with willfulness. God's will, God's yearning, God's wanting will always contradict ours. This perception may be true in the early stages of the conversion process when our wills are not aligned with God's. Beyond the beginnings, however, our wills tend to coincide with God's.

Perhaps we have interpreted God's will as something akin to the will of authorities, mostly those who have impressed us with the fact that only their wishes counted. In order to survive we may have had to put our own desires aside in order to satisfy theirs. Some people have an even more troubling history of parental or educational discipline in which, as children, their will was broken through punishment inflicted by an authority. This disciplining into submission was often presented to the child as God's will. Directors need to be aware of the effects of such negative experiences ascribed to God's will and gently bring them to the surface in order to open a new possibility for the directee.

The following exercise might be helpful for your reflection:

> When was the last time you asked yourself what you really want? And how long did you allow yourself to entertain that longing? Thirty seconds? A couple of minutes? What inner or outer voices suggested that whatever it was, you ought not be so foolish as to think it could be satisfied? At some point, did you judge yourself to be willful or selfish?

Those who have transmitted Christian tradition often neglected the deeper dimensions of the reality of God's yearning and ours beyond the beginnings of spiritual development. Once we awaken to God's love and respond, there is usually a deep stream of mutual desiring going on—a responsive yearning and desiring that is, in fact, one with God's yearning. Once we or our directees go through spiritual awakening, our wills and God's will tend to come together into one yearning, such as Mechtild describes. Increasing intimacy with God actually heals our disordered and misplaced willfulness, gradually transforming it into willingness...openness...spaciousness. The recognition of this process marks the beginning of discovering the convergence of divine and human love that is the actual ground of all our yearnings.

If we mistakenly assume we can't ever have our desires satisfied, then we're pretty close to extinguishing them. We have never discovered where they lead or what might really make us happy. Instead, we attempt to satisfy ourselves. We bury our inchoate, unformed, barely perceptible longings for intimacy with God by settling for whatever forms of consumer goods or relationships are immediately available or convenient. Too often we assuage our wanting with something that can never satisfy the depth of our longings. The interaction we truly desire takes place on a totally different plane; no thing, no human relationship can bear the weight of our longing for God.

North American culture constantly bombards us with advertising through the media. The advertising industry is extraordinarily skilled at manipulating our desire through subliminal messages that tell us what we *ought* to want. They seduce us into thinking we can become secure, safe, and comfortable through consumer goods. The right car, perfume, or deodorant offers happiness or salvation. Lest we think we are uninfluenced by this bombardment, consider that the average person sees or hears a thousand ads per day. A moment's reflection can surface the slogans of particular products in a second. We live in a culture that programs our desires toward *things* rather than toward other values. These artificially created and orchestrated desires direct us away from our own interiority and away from any form of pain or discomfort. It may take some time and sorting out to discover what we want from the inside.

Engaging Our Desires

The Exercises or any other serious interaction with God in prayer that encourages us to entertain and engage our desires is one of the most helpful and growth-enhancing things we can do. It is my experience that such engagement frequently requires the support and encouragement of a spiritual director. It often feels frightening and disconcerting to discover that we don't know what we want or to find that we don't want something badly enough to make the choices it would require. As each thing we *think* we want emerges, it takes some time to test out whether we really do want it or not. This interior sorting through requires listening to ourselves at deeper levels than many of us are accustomed. Consequently, engagement with God and our desires in prayer involves a patient and often lengthy process of tutoring and ordering our desires This takes place only in and through our concrete interaction with God.

Honest prayer, in fact, structures our desires. It is often true that we may not know what we want and that we may often pray for the wrong things, even "snatching at God as at a brass ring." In allowing our desires room to be—to become conscious, intelligent, and available to us, even to become enlarged and expanded—and in the process of praying we find that we and our desires "get sorted out." By following Ignatius's lead, focusing our desires, and praying for specific graces, we often discover more clearly what we don't want and what we do as we continue our dialogue with God.

The book *Primary Speech* by Ann and Barry Ulanov has a wonderful little chapter entitled "Prayer and Desire." As good psychologists, they describe prayer as primary speech—our fantasies, self-talk, conscious and unconscious yearnings. By giving expression to them in the freedom of prayer, if we have come to trust God, we are changed and so too is the shape of our desiring:

> Desire leads to more desire. Prayer articulates our longing for a fullness of being, our reaching out of the mind for what is beyond it, and helps us find and love God and grow with our love. It is like the sun warming a seed into life, like the work of clearing away weeds and bringing water to the interior garden of St. Teresa's inspired imagery. Prayer enlarges our desire until it receives God's desire for us. In prayer we grow big enough to house God's desire for us, which is the Holy Spirit. [3]

Earlier in the same chapter they assert:

> ...God does not need to be told anything about what we need and want. Our words in prayer are not for God's instruction but our own. We discover this way what in fact we do desire, what we want to reach out to and love. Thus we come to hold in open awareness what before we had lived unknowingly.
>
> Surprises happen. We may discover we want more than we thought we dared. In the secret space of prayer, we may reveal to ourselves how much we want truth, beauty, love. In daily life, we usually hide from such desires, trying to protect ourselves from their urgency with the cynical argument that those are merely childish hopes that life correctly disillusions. We may discover desires we did not know about or knew only dimly, desires that if followed would take us far off the path we have so carefully constructed. We might have to change jobs, leave relationships, forsake our whole way of living to take up an entirely different one. Following desires does not, as critics might warn, necessarily lead

to self-indulgence and all the hedonist sensations. Rather, it heads straight into the dangers of moral dilemma. The voice that God hears in prayer gets louder and louder for us if we go on praying. It may come to speak of a truth and a way of life that break sharply with the life we are living.[4]

We have good reason for refusing to entertain our desires. It excuses us from moving toward them. When Ignatius asks us to "pray for what we desire" and then goes on to specify, for example, that we pray "for intimate knowledge of our Lord, who has become a human person for me, that I may love him more and follow him more closely,"[5] we often discover that there is some part of this desire that we don't want, at least not yet. If, as the Ulanovs explain, desire leads to conversion of life, we and our directees may manifest considerable resistance to discovering them or praying for certain graces.

Storyteller Megan McKenna captures this reluctance to claim and act on our desires in a wonderful parable:

There was a woman who wanted peace in the world and peace in her heart and all sorts of good things, but she was very frustrated. The world seemed to be falling apart. She would read the papers and get depressed. One day she decided to go shopping, and she went into a mall and picked a store at random. She walked in and was surprised to see Jesus behind the counter. She knew it was Jesus, because he looked just like the pictures she'd seen on holy cards and devotional pictures. She looked again and again at him, and finally she got up her nerve and asked, "Excuse me, are you Jesus?" "I am." "Do you work here?" "No," Jesus said, "I own the store." "Oh, what do you sell in here?" "Oh, just about anything!" "Anything?" "Yeah, anything you want. What do you want?" She said, "I don't know." "Well," Jesus said, "feel free, walk up and down the aisles, make a list, see what it is you want, and then come back and we'll see what we can do for you."

> She did just that, walked up and down the aisles. There was peace on earth, no more war, no hunger or poverty, peace in families, no more drugs, harmony, clean air, careful use of resources. She wrote furiously. By the time she got back to the counter, she had a long list. Jesus took the list, skimmed through it, looked up at her and smiled. "No problem." And then he bent down behind the counter and picked out all sorts of things, stood up, and laid out the packets. She asked, "What are these?" Jesus replied, "Seed packets. This is a catalog store." She said, "You mean I don't get the finished product?" "No, this is a place of dreams. You come and see what it looks like, and I give you the seeds. You plant the seeds. You go home and nurture them and help them grow and someone else reaps the benefits." "Oh," she said. And she left the store without buying anything.[6]

Like the woman in the parable, we are willing to leave our desire-seeds in the package right in the store. We are unwilling to change or to boldly move toward meeting God in that desire and fulfilling it together. Writer and spiritual director Patrick Carroll suggests, "If I can really discover what I want at the deep level, God wants exactly that. God is not making up stuff for me. God is creating me out of my desire and my moving toward that."[7]

Many of us are not at all sure of what we really want. Yet our desires are present and condition all of our behavior consciously and unconsciously. Since they are there anyway, we might as well let our desires into our prayer and allow them (and in the process, ourselves) to get sorted out. My understanding is that the process is something like this:

> If we receive the courage to voice our desires, the dialogue with Jesus or God can influence, correct, or illumine the misunderstood desire. Praying in such a way that we allow ourselves to be affected by God opens us to influence, to discovery, and to change. We keep on expressing our real desires until they are

fulfilled, until they are changed, or until we are convinced God is responding to us.

The apostle Paul illustrates this process. He tells us, "A thorn was given me in the flesh....Three times, I besought the Lord about this, that it should leave me; but he said to me, 'My grace is sufficient for you, for my power is made perfect in weakness' " (2 Cor 12:8–9). In the relationship, Paul discovered he did not actually need to be delivered from this particular suffering. Something else was going on that was more important. Whether he prayed three times or fifty times about something, his desire was made known, prayed into, and responded to. What he wanted was modified by God's response. Paul's attitude and self-knowledge changed through this interaction and mutual influence.

Here I am discussing fundamental desires, not something we superficially want that really doesn't matter much, but something more like the directionality of our whole being. These deeper desires are more connected to our authenticity, to the kinds of persons we are becoming under the sway of God's grace. These are the desires that result in vocation, a fundamental calling to express our Christian call to share God's life in and through Christ in some concrete way.

In the context of the Exercises and other forms in Christocentric prayer, the person of Jesus, his life, ministry, teaching, death, and resurrection play a central role in shaping and clarifying desires. A personal relationship with Jesus tends to take on a life of its own. As unitive and affective prayer deepen, Jesus begins to live in Christians in ways that concretely help them to know and live out their desires. Disciples are constantly contemplating Jesus—who he is, what he values, and how he acts. Gradually, we desire to share that life, those values, and actions more deeply and with greater constancy.

19

There are many intermediate stages and meanderings in appropriating the mystery of Christian life and of gradually becoming "Jesus" kinds of persons. We discover our need for healing in a relationship that reveals our inability to respond to another's love. We find ourselves in need of reconciliation, confronted with a form of sinfulness we feel helpless to repair. We find we need an infusion of love because we are so limited in our loving that we cannot love someone we want to or feel we should.

At the same time, we may be afraid of the very thing we want. If we've been ill a long time, we may prefer to be invalids rather than assume responsibility for caring for ourselves. We may not wholeheartedly want healing. We may recognize we need to forgive someone to release ourselves from bitterness or resentment about some injury, but we discover we are still angry, and our anger makes us feel strong. We don't want to let it go. So what do we do?

I find it is helpful (in my personal prayer and as a suggestion for directees) to pray for the desire to forgive or to pray for the desire to let go of the anger. The basic principle is emotional congruence. We uncover and express our honest desires. If we can *want* to release anger, for instance, we have become open to a possibility in grace that is not yet ours. Eventually, we can choose to release the anger. We can only pray from our actual feelings, coming to prayer from that honest fundamental desire, which leaves us open to an unpredictable outcome. Praying with this kind of emotional congruency gives great freedom. We can pray out of our anger, our weariness, our discouragement, our fear, our loss, our joy, and so on. We express those feelings to their conclusion or until we're tired of them. When we're finished, we wait for a response. Gradually, we discover changes in us. A Gospel pericope discloses a new possibility. God touches us through another. A long walk by the ocean crying or shouting calms us and we are now open to influence.[8]

This process requires that we and our directees be deeply present to ourselves, to feelings, to the deep places where both the surrender and the withholding are. When we enter into this dialogue, "We discover what in fact we do desire, what we want to reach out and love."[9]

The spiritual direction conversation is a privileged place where the subtle interplay of desire and complex emotional responses can be uncovered and the directee then encouraged to return to prayer with greater understanding, self-knowledge, and self-presence. When we explore with directees or retreatants what they are actually feeling, wanting, and experiencing, we can help them reframe their experience so they can return to pray from the sense of themselves that has emerged in the spiritual direction conversation.

Conditioned Desires

Gerald May gives a wonderful example of how opaque our desires are, even to ourselves. We think we want things that our culture encourages us to want, and sometimes we fail to recognize our deeper desires are already being fulfilled.

> I asked a young woman what she most deeply wanted. She responded immediately, "I'd like a happy home and family, security, a sense of being worthwhile." Then I asked her to sit in silence for a moment and try to be open to what desires she could really *feel*, right in the present moment. After a while she looked up with tears in her eyes. "I don't know what to say. What I actually feel is that things are really okay right now. Better than okay. I don't think I want anything more than what I have at this very moment." I asked her to be still once again, to look more deeply into her present feeling, to seek any desire that might honestly be there. Softly, she said, "It's very hard to put into words. I feel really blessed, and I feel gratitude; I want to say thank you to someone.

Is it God? If it is, I want to give God a hug and say thanks. And I wish people could feel this way more, could have some peace."[10]

May suggests that this woman's first response came from her adjusted, conditioned conception of herself. She first recounts what advertising and culture tell her she is supposed to want. As she became aware of her present-moment feeling, she drew closer to the response of her heart to that reality. Her authentic desire revealed itself to her.[11] This is a wonderful example of how the spiritual direction conversation assists us in discovering our authentic desires.

When we consider "conditioned" responses, it is important to realize that religious people can have a set of responses that are conditioned by their religious culture. The desires we are called to pray for can become routinized. In the *Spiritual Exercises* of St. Ignatius, for instance, the retreatant is invited to:

- ask for a growing and intense sorrow and tears for my sins;
- beg for a deep sense of the pain which the lost suffer, that if because of my faults I forget the love of the eternal Lord, at least the fear of falling into sin;
- ask of our Lord the grace not to be deaf to His call, but prompt and diligent to accomplish His most holy will;
- ask for an intimate knowledge of our Lord, who has become man for me, that I may love Him more and follow Him more closely;
- ask for knowledge of the deceits of the rebel chief and help to guard myself against them; and also to ask for a knowledge of the true life exemplified in the sovereign and true Commander, and the grace to imitate Him;
- beg for the grace to choose what is more for the glory of His Divine Majesty and the salvation of my soul;

- beg God our Lord to deign to move my will, and to bring to my mind what I ought to do in this matter that would be more for His praise and glory;
- ask for sorrow, compassion, and shame because the Lord is going to His sufferings for my sins;
- ask for sorrow with Christ in sorrow, anguish with Christ in anguish, tears and deep grief because of the great affliction Christ endures for me;
- ask for the grace to be glad and rejoice intensely because of the great joy and the glory of Christ our Lord.[12]

These desires can become yet another set of externally generated "oughts" or "shoulds" that we feel we should—but which perhaps we don't really—want. A retreatant, for example, thinks she *ought* to really want to suffer more, but she isn't really interested in that. Going through the motions without much heart results in boring prayer. If we or our directees focus prayer through one of these bogus desires, usually not much will happen.

Sometimes, however, the directee develops real resistance to the proposed desire and even content of a meditation. If this resistance goes unrecognized, attempts to pursue the proposed material will result in taking the retreatant further and further away from his or her own present reality and feeling and the way God wishes to reveal God's self. Those directing the Exercises need to explore with directees if the proposed focus is something that they really desire. If it isn't, then directors need to redescribe or reframe both the desire and the material for meditation in ways that will facilitate prayer. Sometimes directees themselves intuitively sense how God is choosing to reveal God's self to them.

Clarification of Feelings and Desires

If we are working with directees in subsequent retreats or in ongoing direction, the clarification of feelings and especially desires is one of the most important things we can pursue. The way Ignatius structures the sequence of desires presupposes that the person so engaged in the Exercises is undergoing a conversion process—one that usually occurs in the early stages of spiritual awakening. This sequence of desires is also expressed in the metaphors typical of masculine consciousness, which is shaped by the hero's journey and begins with heroic ideals and quests and ends in intimacy in the latter stages. Women's process is a little more complex. For many women, life is in the details rather than in the heroic dream. Desire for women is frequently related to intimate relating. Their desires may or may not be particularly heroic in tone. Nevertheless, Ignatius's schema can have the positive effect of enlarging a woman's desire beyond the constraints of conventional femininity—of inviting her to dream a larger reality for herself.

Specification of Desire for Women

It is important to recognize that Ignatius's principle of "asking for what we desire" can be distinguished from the specific desires he enumerates. I have experimented with expanding the range of those desires through some of the themes in the writing of women mystics. The *Spiritual Exercises* of St. Gertrud, for example, intrigue me as an alternative set of focusing desires that appear to be particularly congruent for women maturing in their intimacy with Christ or God.

Gertrud's exercises are expressed in images drawn from sacramental life and female Benedictine monastic life. In her *Exercises*, Gertrude

- offers an exercise on *rebirth*—the desire to be reborn in God through the holiness of new life and to be restored to a kind of spiritual infancy related to the experience of baptism;
- discusses the desire for *spiritual conversion*, which is related to a core value in Benedictine monasticism. (One is to become God's own "monastery," the dwelling place of love and of all the virtues, literally to house God's love in her being);
- invites her retreatant to the *spiritual marriage*, with exercises awakening love in mutual cherishing;
- recalls her religious profession in the image of *consecration*, her way of following Christ, through the fiercest of desires and prayer;
- explores the idea of *mystical union*, joining oneself to God in affection, devotion, longing, and intention;
- offers exercises in *jubilation*, utter praise of the Divine, anticipating eternity, when she will be satisfied fully by the presence of the Lord;
- concludes with an exercise about *making amends*, confident in the redeeming grace of Jesus.[13]

Contemporary readers may find her language too effusive for their taste, but I like the images whereby she couches these exercises and desires as ways of "enlarging" and making one bolder in desiring. I don't think we pay enough attention to some of her themes, such as jubilation. When was the last time you or your directees spent a whole day exulting in joy in sheer praise of God?

Gertrud ends her exercises with *making amends*. Repentance and contrition emerge in the face of God's mercy and cherishing love. Ignatius, on the other hand, begins here. Are these mystics addressing retreatants at different stages of the spiritual life? Or might these be gendered differences? The themes of these exercises have a distinctively feminine cast to them and expand the imaginative potential of director and directee for recognizing a broader range of spiritual experience than those named by any single mystical writer.

Patrick Carroll provides a contemporary example highlighting the emergence of a focusing desire from a woman's starting place in retreat. He emphasizes the importance of encouraging retreatants to specify for themselves the general desire with which they make the Exercises. What might the particular grace be for this directee? One retreatant focused her entire retreat on how Jesus loves with a mother's love. For this mother, it meant a quality of loving that enabled one to love other people and at the same time to leave them free, even as they are loved with real passion. This freedom to expand the possible desires beyond Ignatius's list of ten allows room for congruently gendered desires to enter into an Ignatian approach to prayer. Directors need to be able to imagine such capacious and novel images and desires as they emerge in their directees as well as to encourage those who might be stuck in conventional images and desires to move toward their own originality and specificity.

Progression of Desire

Gerald May describes a simple progression that begins with desire, moves to intention, and ends with control. He writes: "Desire is wanting something, longing for some satisfaction. Intention is claiming the wanting, consciously owning it, and choosing to seek satisfaction. Control is what we are able to do to make the satisfaction happen."[14] May believes that many need to expand the space between desire and intention, suggesting that too often we leap to control, where we may enjoy only limited success. But like the Ulanovs, he urges us to give our desire space, to allow it room to be free and become enlarged.

This, he suggests, can lead eventually to a whole new way of being and living that stays quite close to God and God's loving, which opens up to us in this process. Claiming our wanting, becoming conscious and choosing it, holds us open to God's desiring and ours becoming one.

The following example from an actual spiritual direction session might make some of these reflections on desire and the process of spiritual direction in relationship to them more concrete.

Susan:	I was doing a guided imagery meditation on the retreat for our women. I really wanted something to happen. Maybe when someone else led the meditation, something more would happen. All I felt was this vague consoling sense of presence. It was peaceful, but I felt frustrated afterwards.
Director:	(Initiates some exploration of what this was like, especially the vagueness, and what prayer was like when she didn't have any images.)
Susan:	It is just kind of peaceful...something of a bare sense of presence.
Director:	When prayer is like that, do you usually feel frustrated?
Susan:	No, usually not.
Director:	What had you been praying with before you went on the retreat?
Susan:	Remember, I'd been praying that Jesus would show me his face. You even gave me Ellen's painting of a face of Jesus to be with in prayer.

Director: Can you tell me a little bit about what was happening in your daily prayer?

Susan: I had the face of Christ painting on the coffee table in my apartment and I would lie down on my couch in a relaxed way facing the window. I have a stained-glass piece hanging in the window that catches the light. But I felt too unprotected when I stretched out on the couch, and I would find my body wanting to crunch up (demonstrates body position, drawing up her knees to her chest).

Director: As you prayed in your apartment, do you remember what you wanted from God?

Susan: Oh, yes, I wanted greater intimacy with God. You know, and I wanted to experience more intense feel-ings in prayer. And I wanted to see God's face. I wanted God to reveal God's self to me again.

Director: Were there any other feelings you were aware of besides these specific longings?

Susan: Well, I want the intimacy, but I'm probably a little bit afraid of it. I don't know if I'm going to feel comfortable if God got really close to me...

Director: Can you bring me up to date a little bit on what's happening in therapy right now?

Susan: Well, therapy is a little bit like my prayer. I am on something of a plateau right now. I feel like I'm on the threshold of something, but I'm not there yet.

Director: Every change in your relationship with God doesn't necessarily mean pain and discomfort. The last several months, you have had a consistent experience

of consolation although your feelings are not particularly intense. What might you feel God wants
for you right now?

Susan: Maybe just for me to relax and be just where I am
for a while in this in-between place.

Director: How would God be with you in that way?

Susan: (She curled up her body into a sitting fetal position,
and just experienced God with her.)

Director: Could God be with you in your fear, just like Jesus
was with the disciples locked up in the upper room?

Susan: Yes, the way Jesus could just come through that
locked door?

Director: In your prayer, could you imagine allowing God to
touch both your fear of intimacy and your desire for
intimacy?

Susan: (She enters a visual meditation in the director's
presence and describes what is happening.) I see
the darkened rooms. The shades and curtains are
drawn. They open. The light is streaming in...

Director: In your curled up posture, how might God be with
you?

Susan: A beautiful woman appears with long, curly hair
and voluminous robes. She folds her robes around
me. I feel her embracing me gently from behind...

Director: (Waits for her to come out of the contemplation.)
You might want to stay with these images in your

prayer for a while. Just let God embrace you gently
from behind and see what happens.[15]

When we as directors ask directees or retreatants to pray
for what they want, I do not think we will be very helpful to
them if we don't assist them in getting beneath their conditioned responses. In this example, Susan is looking for something that blocks her awareness of God's actual presence and
consolation. She failed to notice how God was already becoming more intimate with her. She wasn't, however, clearly aware
that she both wanted to see God's face and was also too fearful
to receive that grace. When Susan was able to express and discover her need to be somewhat self-protective (curled up), she
discovered God was relating to her in a tender and gentle way.
God seemed to be responding to her desire for intimacy, yet
content to embrace her from behind in a way that let her feel
safe. She discovered the deeper place where God was already
arousing her desire for Love itself and experienced union with
that Divine Presence. God met her in a surprising way.

FOR FURTHER REFLECTION:

- In your experience either as a spiritual director or
  directee, how do you pray for what you want?
- What internal or external voices do you need to quiet
  in order to discover your own authentic desire?
- How have you sorted out your desires and been sorted
  out by them?
- What happens with your directees when you encourage them to continue expressing their feelings until
  they discover their core desires and resistances?

NOTES

1. *Beguine Spirituality*, ed. Fiona Bowie, trans. Oliver Davies (New York: Crossroad, 1990), I. 4; I.24; 55–56.

2. *The Spiritual Exercises of St. Ignatius*, trans. Louis J. Puhl (Chicago: Loyola University Press, 1951), no. 48.

3. Ann and Barry Ulanov, *Primary Speech: A Psychology of Prayer* (Atlanta: John Knox Press, 1982), 20. The phrase "sorting out our desires" is theirs.

4. Ibid., 17.

5. *Exercises*, no. 104.

6. Megan McKenna, *Parables: The Arrows of God* (Maryknoll, N.Y.: Orbis Press, 1994), 28–29.

7. L. Patrick Carroll, in response to the oral presentation of this material in Portland, Oregon, August 9, 1995. I am grateful for his influence in developing this version of the material.

8. Interviews I collected for a current research project verified that for those who pray in this expressive way, it was a common pattern for interviewees to vent their feelings or chat with Jesus or God. After the expression, if they stayed in prayer, they first came to a peaceful pause when either they began to view their own situation differently or they began to sense God affecting them.

9. Ulanovs, *Primary Speech*, 17.

10. Gerald May, *The Awakened Heart: Living Beyond Addiction* (San Francisco: Harper, 1991), 50.

11. Ibid., 50.

12. *Exercises*, nos. 55, 65, 92, 104, 139, 152, 180, 193, 203, 221.

13. See *Gertrud the Great of Helfta: Spiritual Exercises*, trans. Gertud Jaron Lewis and Jack Lewis, Cistercian Fathers Series, 49 (Kalamazoo: Cistercian Publications, 1989). Each of these "exercises" appears as a chapter in this work.

14. May, *Awakened Heart*, 54–56.

15. Used with the permission of the directee.

Chapter 2

ENDLESSLY INVENTIVE EVASION: RESISTANCE IN SPIRITUAL DIRECTION

In his excellent treatment of resistance, psychiatrist and spiritual director Gerald May observes: "The human mind is an endless source of inventiveness when it comes to avoiding the implications of spiritual experience."[1] Avoidance aptly suggests the psychoanalytic phenomenon of resistance, in this instance, as it occurs in relationship to our spiritual lives. Resistance can be defined as an unconscious response that is part of all normal growth in which the person avoids some issue, some experience, or some insight by some form of avoiding behavior. It is caused by the ambivalence we all feel toward change in another or ourselves.

After many years of personal prayer and of spiritual direction with others, I am inclined to make an even stronger assertion than May: Most of us are engaged in endlessly inventive evasion not only of the *implications* of spiritual experience, but often, and more confusingly, of the experiences of God that we claim to desire. God gently lures us into intimacy and unexpectedly explodes us into mystery. Such encounters with mystery are simply too much for most of us until our capacity expands and our tolerance increases over the course of our spiritual development. Most of us lose our nerve somewhere between the lure and the explosion. As T. S. Eliot wrote in the *Four Quartets*, "…human kind/Cannot bear very much reality." Paul Tillich put it slightly differently and sympathetically: "If you've never run away from your God, I wonder who your God is." Evasion is directly related to both the closeness of God's approach to us and to our instinctive withdrawal from God's presence. Experiences of God as mystery evoke awe, even fear, in the face of the numinous and uncontrollable otherness of God.

This dynamic of fear of and flight from intimacy with God—the holiness of God, the unpredictability of God, and even the tenderness of God—occurs because our small, conditioned sense of self is threatened in both obvious and subtle ways by such encounters. The *Spiritual Exercises* of St. Ignatius consist of a pedagogy for progressively learning to live more intimately and consistently in the mystery of God's love for us. The Exercises evoke and nurture, when rightly experienced, a profound conversion experience. Subsequently, they seek to stabilize retreatants so they might continue to develop an increasing capacity to bear more grace, to become more God-filled, and thus to become so God-possessed that God can act in the world in and through them. This ongoing process extends well beyond the experience of the retreat itself and ripens over a lifetime. Frequently this process finds particular expression in successive retreat experiences.

This developmental mystical process consists of continued, successive transformations. Nothing is ever the same again once we and our directees begin to surrender to God and commit ourselves to traverse the entire path. Whenever we glimpse a potential need to change, most of us find a convenient way to avoid the agent or circumstances of that change. All our defenses arise, not because we so choose, but because we are naturally self-protective of our present sense of self and way of life. This is not necessarily willful or even conscious. Consequently, directors need to understand these dynamics thoroughly. They simply happen, and our response as directors can make an enormous difference in our directees' lives.

Resistance is a technical psychological term that aptly accounts for these endlessly varied and subtle responses. Nevertheless, it is not a term we as directors should ever use with directees. Should we accusingly ask our directees, "Why are you resisting?", a likely response could be even greater defensiveness. Resistance, though, can be a helpful concept through which to identify and reflect on some very typical experiences all of us have both as directors and as pray-ers.

Resistance in Spiritual Direction

As defined above, resistance constitutes unconscious avoidance. Our ambivalence about change in another or ourselves accounts for these subtle reactions. Like Susan in the verbatim that ended Chapter 1, we are often unaware of the fear that prevents us from claiming and intending what we desire. Although we want, for instance, greater intimacy with God as Susan did, we are also unwilling or not yet ready for the way our lives might change were God to fulfill that desire. We often want a change that we are not entirely willing to implement. Most of us find changing our behavior or our commitments threatening.

By definition, everyone resists at some time or another. This resistance is entirely *unconscious* so we can't help it until it becomes conscious. The intensity and depth of this avoidance admits of degrees: mild, moderate, or serious.[2] This notion of degrees is extremely important for spiritual directors who may not be trained clinicians. In her direction session, Susan's willingness to explore the block she was experiencing in prayer indicated that her level of resistance was quite mild. Once Susan could recognize her fear of the very intimacy with God she also wanted, she was able to relax. Susan was sufficiently relaxed during the session that she could allow God to be with her in her fear. The ability of a directee to respond to such an exploration of potential resistance confirms for the director the appropriateness and timeliness of gently working with this material. With the help of her director, Susan was able to move toward her desire for greater intimacy with God in a way she could not when she was alone and unaware of her fear.

Within the context of therapy or psychoanalysis (from which this concept emerged), resistance usually refers to avoidance of something the therapist wants to address with a counselee. The therapist usually feels it immediately and directly. As I adopt and apply the unconscious dynamics referred to by this term, I identify three distinct ways in which the dynamics of *resistance* are experienced within the spiritual direction conversation.

Resistance to Spiritual Experience

The first form resistance takes in spiritual direction is directees' avoidance of religious experience itself. The spiritual direction conversation focuses on the directee's relationship with God. When directees avoid something in this relationship, their avoidance has nothing to do with the director; it is part of the God-human relationship. Directees frequently move away from God's inbreak into their lives because something about the experience frightens them. This *something* might be the surprise of God's initiation in the relationship, the intensity of God's presence, the directee's affective response, a perceived threat to self-image, a change in the way prayer is experienced, or a sense that unpleasant or undesirable consequences will follow. Any of these might result in a countermovement. God draws close and the directee finds a way to flee. The following narrative illustrates resistance to some aspect of the directee's relationship with God.

> Sister Grace, in her early twenties and contemplating making final vows in her community, wondered how the women ahead of her in the formation process could be sure they were ready to make this commitment. One Saturday morning, she was discussing this with a friend who was planning to make final vows in a few months. Her friend said to her, "Have you tried asking God about this?" Grace replied, "I hadn't thought about that," and actually went to her room to pray. When she prayed, asking if God wanted her to make final vows, she experienced her bedroom suddenly filled with light, more than the sun streaming through the windows could account for. And she felt deeply loved by God. However, this surprisingly immediate response to her prayer and the intensity of God's love and presence frightened her and she fled her room.
>
> Her friend noticed her pacing one of the corridors and commented, "I thought you said you were going to pray." Grace responded, "I did, and God is in my room right now!" Her friend asked the next logical question, "Then what are you doing out here? Don't you think you should go back?" Grace replied, "I've got enough of an answer for now!" She did go back to her room, and the light had faded. The overwhelming palpable sense of God's presence and love was no longer there.[3]

In this example, Sister Grace's friend models excellent spiritual direction skills. She focuses Grace on a direct encounter with God as the basis for her decision making. When Grace prays with this intention, she receives far more than she expected. God's response is clear and unmistakable, at least in terms of God's inviting her to an ongoing relationship. Grace realizes that this epiphany already indicates pretty clearly the direction in which God is inviting her. But she is neither totally ready to welcome the implications of that invitation nor able at this moment to remain present to God in the face of this awesome and loving numinosity. She physically leaves. But when her friend challenges her, she receives the support she needs to return to prayer and does so. Had her friend not met her at that moment, she might not have returned to prayer and may have even forgotten to mention this experience in a later spiritual direction conversation.

In the silent, enclosed retreat, dynamics such as those in the previous narrative are usually fairly evident to the director. Directees who become self-reflective will also notice these responses, perhaps after the fact, and yet often feel helpless to do any better. In Grace's case, she abruptly ended the experience by physically leaving her room. There are many more subtle ways of slowing down, moving away from, or stopping the intimate communication of God with a directee. One reason spiritual direction proves so helpful, especially during a retreat process, lies in a director's ability to recognize when the directee is moving away from the spiritual experience being offered. Gently helping the directee return to prayer and receive the intimacy or grace being offered supports the directee's development.

Within the process of the Exercises, a retreatant may develop resistance to a particular exercise rather than to what is transpiring between the directee and God. In this case, the director needs to invite the retreatant to move to the next theme or process only when he or she is graced with the readiness to do so. Expressed repugnance to a particular theme or exercise usually indicates that the timing is off. Typically, the next movement appears spontaneously in the directee's prayer before the director introduces it. This preliminary emergence of content or affective disposition suggests the appropriateness of proceeding. If the director moves faster than the directee's prayer can support, the directee is likely to develop resistance both to the director and to the process of the Exercises.

Resistance to Prayer

In the nineteenth annotation retreat, sometimes called the retreat in daily life, avoidance of spiritual experience or of the Jesus-retreatant relationship often manifests itself in the directee's not having time to pray, becoming too busy, or finding some way to avoid the practice of prayer itself. In this case, it is important for the director to have background information about the particular directee. Some people have never developed a sufficiently disciplined life to engage in a regular rhythm of prayer in their daily round. The retreat in daily life creates a structure that supports developing such a discipline as well as fostering conversion and greater intimacy with Jesus. These directees will need considerable help in objectively reflecting on their life situations and problem-solving the obstacles that seem to prevent this regular, sustained practice of prayer. For instance, what might the retreatant actually choose to do during the time supposedly set aside for prayer? Clean the refrigerator? Read the paper? Flip on the TV? Do any of these activities have to be done at that moment? Similar dynamics around the practice of prayer may also occur in somewhat less intense forms in ongoing spiritual direction apart from the retreat in daily life.

A directee with an already established discipline of regular prayer presents another case. Like Sister Grace in the previous narrative, such a directee may be slowing down the developing intimacy with God or avoiding some aspect of the prayer experience itself, such as feeling overwhelmed or out of control in the face of its intensity.

Yet another way resistance to the practice of prayer manifests itself occurs when a person continues to pray but attempts to maintain control of the experience of prayer by method, conditions, or expectations. Some directees attracted to the practice of centering prayer or the method of mantra meditation taught by John Main, for example, will continue to focus on their sacred word and ignore all other contents or activities of God in their prayer. The person praying continues with their favorite method despite what God might be doing! Both of these methods of prayer, which are very appropriate for many directees at various times in their prayer lives, may actually be used as defenses against feelings that the directee may not wish to experience.

Other directees read descriptions of prayer that favor a simple sense of being in God's presence without feeling or content and decide not to notice any content that is present. In this case, prayer is reported to be somewhat flat, maybe even boring, with nothing much happening. A more global resistance to God or to something emerging in oneself is masked by avoidance behavior around the practice and processes of prayer. Directees may simply go through the motions and not really make themselves available to God in prayer, or they may not get around to prayer at all and just not deal with what is being avoided. As this condition continues, such people frequently become more and more irritable, uncomfortable, and affectively distanced from God and from themselves.

Frequently, directees resist prayer experiences in order to avoid uncomfortable feelings, unpleasant memories, and unflattering insights about themselves. They may perhaps feel too vulnerable (victims of abuse) or out of control (adult children of alcoholics/abuse). They may sense that a change or conversion of life might be required, or they may be overwhelmed by feelings of anger, grief, sexual attraction, jealousy, and other so-called negative emotions. Avoidances in these areas also take on particular coloration depending on gender. Men frequently find it extremely difficult to experience vulnerability and loss of control in prayer. Women are sometimes more comfortable with a range of emotion in prayer but may have difficulties with anger particularly.

In a more positive vein, directees may also resist the confusion that results from the loss of a familiar and predictable way of praying, which often happens when contemplation begins to occur. The loss of treasured God-images, which correspond to out-grown self-images, frequently evokes resistance in the form of nostalgia. No one whom I have accompanied through the transition from discursive prayer into contemplative prayer has failed to resist some aspect of this development; all persisted in returning to forms of prayer that no longer supported or even worked until she or he had grown accustomed to this new experience in prayer.

The concrete form that resistance takes in directees depends on their psychological makeup and the particular psychological defenses they habitually employ in other areas of their lives.[4] One of the most frequent forms of resistance directors will encounter is the unconscious strategy of "forgetting." Either through repression, suppression, or self-distraction, the directee fails to remember the experience either immediately after it occurred or after talking about it in spiritual direction. Usually, the most important aspects of the experience are forgotten so that the experience ceases to invite the directee to respond or act on its implications.

A second example may illuminate some of the dynamics of resistance already described, as well as some yet to be described:

Linda: I'm OK, thanks; busy as ever. Prayer times are
            OK too. Nothing to write home about. I can't say I
            have much to tell you about in that department
            even though I've been pretty consistent at giving
            it some time—most days. In fact, I'm really getting
            BETTER at that! I've set up a routine that's really
            working for me—that hour in the morning.

Director: Sounds as if you're feeling pretty good about yourself for getting that kind of rhythm in your life and being more consistent in prayer.

Linda: uhmm...

Director: When you say that the routine is "working well" for you, what do you mean by that? What's actually going on there?

Linda: Well, the same as always: I take the daily readings, sit with them, and kind of wait for a word or a line to take root.

Director: And has anything taken root?

Linda: (laughing) Well, no. Like I said a few minutes ago, it's been sort of nondescript the past few weeks. But everything's fine as far as prayer goes. I'm just kind of there waiting for a line to take root and that's OK.

Director: It's kind of interesting that you're really talking about your prayer now in a way that's VERY different from the last time we talked. I guess it was only last month.

Linda: I am?? Mmm... yes, I guess I am. Well, you have to expect that it won't always be the same, right?

Director: (pause) Linda, do you REMEMBER what you shared with me the last time?

Linda: (long pause) Vaguely. But that's long time ago now! A whole month. Some pieces are beginning to come back. (pause...and very matter of factly) Yes, I remember now. We talked about how I'd been filled with a surge of love and affection for every member of my family—all of them—suddenly seeing each of them as individual persons held and bathed in God's love.

Director: Yes...and do you know what else I'm remembering? There were tears in your eyes when you were talking about it.

Linda: Hmmmm...

Director: Do you feel any of that now?

Linda: No, not really. It's gone. I mean I REMEMBER it, but I'm not FEELING it anymore.

Director: Do you remember how that happened, or even when the feelings disappeared?

Linda: I don't know (annoyed). You don't expect feelings to stay forever, do you? It happened. It's over. Things are back to normal now.

Director: What's "normal"?

Linda: "Normal" is that I am not tearing up when I meditate. And, (smiling) besides most of my family is driving me crazy again. But that isn't even what I wanted to talk about with you today. Actually, I hear a lot of people talking about "centering prayer" and I was hoping you might teach me about that today.[5]

Resistance to the Spiritual Director or to Spiritual Direction

The second way that resistance emerges in the spiritual direction conversation is through a dynamic occurring between the director and the directee. This resistance may develop in response to the director's ineptitude, obtuseness, or abuse. Directees can develop an aversion to sharing their intimate experiences of God and their unique responses if they feel they are being judged, misunderstood, misinterpreted, or overly controlled by a director. As directors, we do make real mistakes, perhaps challenging a directee before we have earned their trust and confidence. We may be too tired or too distressed about something going on in our own lives to be truly present to the directee, and they sense our absence. Sometimes the interpersonal chemistry may simply not be right between us. Sometimes our timing is off when we choose to explore possible resistance. And sometimes we give subtle physical cues that we aren't "up to anything too heavy" on a given day. All of these things may lead directees to develop some resistance. Our unhelpful responses, ineptitude, or lapses of attentiveness and presence, however, do not comprise the only reasons directees may develop resistance in the spiritual direction conversation.

Skillful spiritual direction conversations may evoke resistance because they focus attention, raise awareness, and make demands for conversion on the directee. The spiritual direction conversation itself is historically a powerful ascetical tool precisely because it requires ongoing consciousness and reflection on the part of directees. The very attempt to articulate subtle and significant religious experience on a regular basis with someone who really listens increases the claim God makes on directees to respond to God and to order or reorder life and decisions in harmony with this developing relationship. Linda's case above demonstrates this aspect of the relationship. The director's allusion to Linda's experience the previous month at least partially stimulated her memory, even though she also avoided letting the resulting implications continue to develop for her.

This resistance to spiritual direction has often puzzled me. Directees who participate in the practicum with supervised interns report how wonderful the experience was but often choose not to continue beyond the six-month contract period. They will say, "This was nice; someone else should get a chance!" Or they will agree to stay in direction at less frequent intervals and then drop out after a session or two. Usually, this is a form of resistance to the ongoing change that regular prayer and subsequent reflection with a director requires. Sometimes this avoidance has nothing to do with the director's skill or presence. Rather, these directees avoid the qualitative commitment to spiritual growth that ongoing spiritual direction facilitates. Some directees simply slow down their own process by withdrawing from spiritual direction.

Another instance of resistance to the spiritual director occurs in response to the very good clarifying questions a director may ask. Linda's mild attack on her director illustrates this: "You don't expect feelings to stay forever, do you?" The director had simply recalled the tender feelings that had accompanied her previous account and had begun to explore when and how this particular consoling experience ended, as Ignatius counsels in the *Exercises*.[6] I have been with directees for six to eight sessions before they were able to say very much about the specific quality and "feel" of their experience in prayer. After several sessions, they usually trust enough to share their experience and have come to expect the invitation to discuss it. At other times, a directee avoids the question by answering a question other than the one asked. Or he or she might abruptly change the topic of conversation in order to end the exploration the director had begun, as Linda does when she brings up centering prayer. Others might respond by projecting onto the director their perception of how God is acting toward them. If their prayer is pretty boring—and hence their descriptions—they will say, "You must be pretty bored with this same old story each time."

The Director's Resistance to Their Directees or Their Religious Experience

The third way resistance emerges derives from the *director's* need to avoid something in the spiritual direction conversation. Just as the directee may directly reject or withdraw from a director, so too, a director may develop avoidant behavior toward a directee or some part of his or her experience. The director, dreading an impending interview, might forget the appointment or arrive late. In such a case, the director may be misinterpreting the directee's resistance to prayer or to God's initiatives as personal rejection. The director may become depressed or discouraged because the directee is making no progress; he or she gets caught in the directee's resistance and becomes affected by it.

Any interpersonal relationship can evoke resistance. This resistance can and does emerge in the spiritual direction relationship, especially if the exigencies of the relationship require change on the part of the director. Maybe a director will have to do more background study to be with this directee. Or if the director is an untreated alcoholic and the directee is successfully in recovery, the director may not want to deal with the directee's threat to the director's system of denial. Or this directee's current situation may require more time or emotional energy than the director has to give.

The way directors sometimes avoid exploring and sharing a woman's pain of exclusion, oppression, anger, depression, and powerlessness provides a classic example of such resistance, especially for those of us who listen to many women today. There are days when a woman director doesn't want to hear one more such story, perhaps because she doesn't want to feel depressed or powerless herself, and so doesn't engage this woman's particular experience. Some men directors find it very difficult to be with a woman's anger. They intuitively sense that without warning they may become the target of this anger, deservedly or undeservedly, simply because they are part of the oppressing system. Women learn very quickly who can be trusted and how much. A constant censoring and adjusting process goes on, depending upon how much the other can hear or bear. If men directors can receive these experiences and do not become resistant and block their empathy, the potential for healing and empowerment is immense.

Avoidance of directees' religious experience comprises an even more serious form of resistance for directors. This may develop, for example, if a director is experiencing a period of darkness or obscurity in prayer and the directee is being gifted with experiences of intimacy, illumination, and vision. In these circumstances, a director may not want to hear about such experiences and may divert attention away from what God is doing with the directee. Sometimes a director may become frightened by the directee's mystical experiences, may be uncomfortable with the use of particular imagery, may simply be in over his or her head, or may be encountering something unfamiliar. Any of these reactions can cause the director to ignore the directee's experience or, worse yet, to deflect the conversation.

In the experience of supervising spiritual directors, the director's tendency to move away from the directee's actual religious experience frequently comes up.[7] For example, one director struggled to maintain interest in his directee's visionary experiences. Although this mode of prayer was not congenial to the director, he had some understanding of it from his own mother's experience. His directee reported that when she had previously tried to talk to a confessor about these religious experiences, he told her to try not to let it happen again! Warned by her narrative, this particular priest-director carefully refused to act on his instinct to dismiss this woman and her experience. In disciplining himself to listen intently and respond carefully to his directee's story, he also felt challenged to deepen his own prayer life. He realized he was avoiding allowing his own prayer to develop. Over time, he could see that his attention to this directee's experiences had a very positive effect on her.

If the directee is also surprised, a little frightened, or unsure about what is happening, the director's collusion in moving away from this experience can negatively affect the directee. The director's resistance to the religious experience will tend to reinforce the directee's fear or anxiety in the face of new experience. Ignatius compares the role of the director to the fulcrum or the "balance point" on a scale. The director's role provides a stabilizing presence so the directee can remain focused on God and God's direct communication. Some balance point the director is if he or she flees the directee's religious experience! Directees often need their directors to hold steady so they can move toward instead of away from experiences. In many cases they could not tolerate such movement without that support. Directors need to help directees recognize how their unique responses weaken or divert them from the grace God is offering, rather than join the directee in avoidance.

It is helpful for directors to pray before and during sessions in order to remain sufficiently connected to God. In this way, they ally themselves with God's activity, seeking support from God in order to help their directees.

The director's resistance to either the directee or to the directee's religious experience and its implications is best dealt with in the process of supervision. It is never appropriate to burden the directee with the director's issues; directees tend to have enough of their own. The director's resistance is often part of the countertransference process, which will be discussed in chapter 6.

Suggestions for Working with Resistance

My remaining reflections focus on what resistance looks like in the directee's responses and how directors can work with it so as not to evoke even greater avoidance. Resistance or avoidance has the effect of slowing down either the process of change or the process of growing intimacy in the God-human relationship. All of us create some ways of avoiding the pain of growth, the challenge of learning new behaviors, the demands of increasing intimacy, of being honest with ourselves, or of uncovering motives, faults, or sin. Change in our images of ourselves or our images of God, the need to stop a specific behavior or characteristic feeling response, or the need to move from insight to decision can all evoke delay.

How might we as directors respond to the directee's resistance or avoidance in spiritual direction? The attitude we take may comprise the most important aspect of our response. If we are honest about our own spiritual growth and our life of prayer, we recognize that despite our various forms of resistance, God ultimately works through it in gentle or dramatic ways. If the directee resists something in his or her relationship with God, then it is really God's responsibility to grace this particular directee uniquely. All of us get frightened when God draws near. We adopt innumerable strategies to feel more in control and less threatened. (Recall the example at the beginning of this chapter, when Sister Grace spontaneously left her room.) God is usually more active and more patient than we are as directors. We need to align ourselves with God's patience, compassion, and gentleness.

We are more able to remain patient, yet alert to resistance, if we remember that resistance is always *unintentional* and *unconscious*. Our directees consequently are not aware at the moment that they are avoiding something. This differs significantly from a directee's willful and conscious refusal to cooperate with God or to act on a decision. One of the greatest services we can render as directors is helping directees become aware of how, when, and perhaps why they are avoiding the God-encounter or the implications of the God-experience. We will develop the necessary delicacy and sensitivity for bringing avoidant behavior into awareness if we learn to expect resistance.

Possible Approaches

- Expect that when God draws unmistakably near, the directee will at some point unconsciously move away, shut down, misinterpret, forget, repress, or deny it. Ignatius describes clearly how the "spirits" work. In the "Rules for Discernment for Week II," one looks at the beginning, middle, and end of a train of thoughts or activities that have the end result of moving away from the consolation.[8] The movements are subtle, and usually the distraction is attraction to another good. If we as directors help directees retrace their train of consciousness beginning with the last incident of consolation, the point of resistance usually manifests itself. Linda's director does just this when she asks her if she remembers what she shared in the last session. Linda at first recalls the details of her experience of being filled with a surge of love and affection for every member of her family without any affect and in a matter-of-fact tone. Her director then recalls the tears Linda shed the first time she had talked about this. Linda persists in her resistance by insisting that things are back to normal. It's over. In contrast to Sister Grace's acting on her friend's suggestions, Linda shows a higher level of resistance to her religious experience. Linda's resistance will demand greater patience and alertness on the director's part in subsequent sessions.

- Approach a directee's resistance with an excess of empathy. After all, is this not a familiar experience of our own? Do not attack either the directee or the resistance. Attack will only evoke a deeper resistance and obscure the directee's initial, usually subtle, avoidance.
- Recognize that you must have already established a positive relationship of trust, empathy, and openness.
- Notice in an open-minded, nonjudgmental way what appears to be going on. Everyone resists some of the time; no one resists all of the time. Observe long enough to be sure avoidance is *real*. Some reactions may be appropriate responses to a director's mistreatment of a directee. All tardiness to sessions is not necessarily resistance to spiritual direction, to you as a spiritual director, or to spiritual experience. Make notes about the pattern in a concrete way. Offer a nonjudgmental description of the pattern you have observed. Finally, explore it from the directee's perspective. Have they ever noticed this? What did it feel like for them? Differentiate between:
     a. resistance to God/or prayer
     b. resistance to a content
     c. a defensive character structure (massive resistance)
     d. resistance between director and directee
- Share the information as you wonder about it with the directee.

Mild or Moderate Resistance

A directee with mild or moderate resistance may be embarrassed but will usually respond positively to the exploration. The verbatim at the end of chapter 1, regarding Susan's desire to see God's face, is such a case. As she discovered a certain self-protectiveness in her body-posture of curling up in the chair, she was able to reenter prayer with that feeling and experience God with her right there. Such a directee will frequently be grateful to the director for noticing such resistance and, with support, can often change a response once he or she understands what is going on.

Depending on what the avoidance is about, directees may need to change the way they are praying, let go of an inadequate theological perspective, welcome the emergence of a new image of God, return to prayer with the feelings they now recognize, or discover what happens now that they are more conscious of a fear, anger, or desire. For some, insight or awareness alone releases a new freedom for response. Others may need the director to help them with problem-solving the "block" that emerged so that, in light of the new information, the directee can return to prayer or to the place of the last consolation.

Massive Resistance

A massively resistant person will become hostile or defensive, may shut down, or may even attack the director! In these instances, we as directors need both patience and humility. We may have been wrong or unskillful. Conversely, we may have been accurate but will need to be very gentle and patient with the directee as we move away from the hoped for insight and test what is possible for this person. In both cases we need to rely on God's gracious presence and guidance to protect us from feeling too devastated and to help us discover what to do next or how to be. If a directee is massively resistant to most interventions a director makes, it may be a sign that this is a larger personality issue, leaving the person unable to respond or change without professional psychological assistance. Directors without clinical training should be extremely careful about directly confronting the resistance in these directees and should seek supervision and consultation for such situations.

Confronting resistance is not without risk. But without learning how to respond and take that risk, directors may either underestimate or overestimate a directee's capacity for growth. The director should have developed a rapport with the directee that enables him or her to sense a directee's receptivity to this level of challenge.

We are, indeed, endlessly inventive in our evasion of spiritual experience. None of us is exempt and neither are our directees. The *Exercises* themselves have a great potential for evoking resistance because of the way they structure the conversion process or because the language and imagery may not suit some retreatants. As directors we can help our directees recognize their typical evasions and, on occasion, move toward God or at least stay with God for increasing periods of time. God, however, meets us right in our ambivalence and our avoidances. God moves close and withdraws; God respects our still-developing capacities; God is more persistent in luring us into intimacy than our responses warrant. We can trust God to help us and our directees to relax our defenses to the point where we can welcome God into our lives more fully and with increasing mutuality.

- In your experience either as a spiritual director or as a directee, recall instances of resistance and how you worked with them.
- As a director, are you aware of the kinds of contents or experiences of directees you instinctively want to avoid?
- How is spiritual direction itself a means of intensifying awareness so that mild resistance is easily and nondefensively noticed?
- How might the image and/or experience of giving birth illuminate the dynamics of resistance?[9]

NOTES

1. Gerald May, *Care of Mind/Care of Spirit* (San Francisco: Harper, 1982), 85.

2. See Michael Cavanaugh, *The Counseling Experience* (Monterey: Brooks/Cole, 1982), 240–63; Gerard Egan, *The Skilled Helper*, 2d edition (Monterey: Brooks/Cole, 1982), 152–55; and May, *Care of Mind/Care of Spirit*, chapters 5 and 6 for helpful descriptions and discussion of resistance. I am following Cavanaugh primarily.

3. Used with permission of the sister.

4. See chapters 5 and 6 of May's *Care of Mind/Care of Spirit* for further descriptions and explanations.

5. This verbatim was fabricated by the staff of Mercy Center, Burlingame, California, for their internship in the Art of Spiritual Direction several years ago and has been much amended since then in successive role-plays.

6. *The Spiritual Exercises of St. Ignatius*, trans. Louis J. Puhl (Chicago: Loyola University Press, 1951) nos. 333.5–334.6.

7. Maureen Conroy uses the terms *movement* and *counter-movement* to discuss whether or not directors or directees are moving toward increasing consolation or away from consolation in their direction sessions and in the directees' prayer. In her analysis, almost any counter-movement could be resistance. See *Looking into the Well: Supervision of Spiritual Directors* (Chicago: Loyola University Press, 1995), 179–80.

8. Ignatius defines spiritual consolation this way: "I call it consolation when an interior movement is aroused in the soul, by which it is inflamed with love of its Creator and Lord, and as a consequence, can love no creature on the face of the earth for its own sake, but only in the Creator of them all. It is likewise consolation when one sheds tears that move to the love of God, whether it be because of sorrow for sins, or because of the sufferings of Christ our Lord, or for any other reason that is immediately directed to the praise and service of God. Finally, I call consolation every increase of faith, hope, and love, and all interior joy that invites and attracts to what is heavenly and to the salvation of one's soul by filling it with peace and quiet in its Creator and Lord." *Exercises*, no. 316.

9. Stacey Cates-Carney developed this parallel with great effect in her response to my initial presentation of this material at the Ignatian Spirituality Institute in August of 1995.

Chapter 3

"PANNING FOR GOLD": ATTENDING TO THEOLOGICAL THEMES IN SPIRITUAL DIRECTION

A spiritual director made this observation in one supervisory session: "Spiritual direction is like panning for gold. A directee comes and together we dip into the stream of their life and pull up all kinds of things. Rocks of all sizes—I can never guess what's coming next—all kinds of conflicts and problems, then all of a sudden some fleck or nugget of pure gold emerges into view in the bottom of the pan as we swirl the water around, emptying out the rocks." This is a powerful and captivating metaphor for the process of spiritual direction. Together, the director and directee look at everything— whatever is in the water and in the pan—during their session. The director receives the directee's life and everything in that life, helping the directee contemplate the gold among all the conflicts and blocks and stuck places. A skillful, graced director gives that gold reverence, time, interest, and attention until the directee realizes how much more valuable and significant are the flecks of gold—the experiences of grace and the Spirit—than are all the stuck or problematic areas of his or her life.

In spiritual direction, we hear incident after incident of grace, of discovery, of struggle. As directors, we persist in gently asking, "Where is God in all of this?" Our directees may become tired of this question, but directors cannot cease looking for the answer in the directee's experience. Proficient directors, relaxed in the spiritual director role, learn to ask this question more with the quality of alert attention than with words, just like the director who saw himself panning for gold. Directors may well glimpse, even before directees, the flecks of gold in today's swishing-through of the streams of their lives and so help their directees to discover those riches, too. These flecks of gold are the directees' experience of Spirit.

This chapter attempts to help directors and their directees reflect on the theological dimensions of spiritual direction, connecting these experiences of Spirit—the gold—to Christian tradition. This theological dimension of spiritual direction includes awareness of the operative theologies of both director and directee, awareness of the director's theology of religious experience and grace, and the director's ability to make connections between the mysteries of Christian faith, as professed by the churches, and the directee's personal experience of those mysteries in daily life. Although this dimension may appear somewhat abstract at first, I hope that by the end of this chapter both directors and their directees might better recognize and more consciously participate in the process of meaning-making that occurs when we interpret our most significant experiences of grace in the light of Christian tradition.

In the spiritual direction context, interpretation and meaning-making most effectively occur after hearing directees' stories. These narratives already include an implicit theology, a particular understanding of the event embedded in the story itself.[1] So, as directees attempt to respond more deeply in prayer and action to the ways God seems to be inviting them, they also need to think critically about those experiences and the ways they understand them. They need to recognize when their experiences of the Spirit require them to develop new, more adequate ways of understanding and articulating their faith—their theology. Theology is nothing more than faith seeking understanding. As adults, we seek such understanding in the light of our psychological development, our experience, and our personalized articulation of faith.[2]

The first section of this chapter discusses operative theologies, which influence the way directors respond to their directees' experiences. Drawing on the experiences of the Spirit as developed by theologian Karl Rahner, I encourage directors to expand their understandings of what *counts* for religious experience in order to recognize and encompass a broader range of possibilities. Secondly, I address the possibility that directors and directees may be operating from different theologies, which may create conflict in spiritual direction. After that, I briefly reflect on the mysteries of Christian faith in order to offer spiritual directors who may not be entirely familiar with professional theology a shorthand way of recognizing theological content in their directees' stories. These mysteries of Christian faith, which appear in our creeds, represent a theological language we share with our directees. Finally, I make some concrete suggestions about how directors might respond to the theological content of their directees' narratives in spiritual direction.

Operative Theologies

Both the spiritual director and the directee are profoundly affected by their operative theologies. What we believe and how we understand that belief influences how we live our spiritual lives and how we interpret our religious experience. An example might help to make the distinction between operative and espoused beliefs.

Thirty-year-old Sister Mary is making her annual retreat. She, like Susan in chapter 1, is seeking greater intimacy with Jesus in her prayer. While on retreat, she discovers through the help of her director that although she believes Jesus is loving, compassionate, and interested in her (her espoused theology), she actually harbors a hidden fear that drawing closer to Jesus will inevitably result in suffering (her operative theology). Her director suggests that her relationship with Jesus might feel different if she stopped approaching it as if she were going to the dentist. When Mary realizes she is operating on a theology other than the one she thinks expresses her belief, she becomes free to act on her espoused theology.

In this case, Mary needed to change her *operative* theology in order to act on her desires. In other cases, directees or directors may need to change their *espoused* theologies to better match the helpful instincts of their operative theologies. And of course, for others, operative and espoused theologies may be in harmony with one another.

Directors and their directees may or may not share similar theological perspectives, which may be due to developmental differences, theological education, or denominational differences. At the same time, they do share the Jesus story and the Christian belief system. The spiritual direction conversation is one arena in which directees notice and reflect on the mysteries of Christian faith as they unfold within their life experience. Christian belief, liturgy, and community comprise the horizon of meaning that influences both the religious experience of the directee and its interpretation.

The operative theologies of spiritual directors may serve either as a limitation or a resource. If our theologies are too limited, we may miss where God is in the stream of life. If we are open to a variety of theological possibilities, our directees' experiences of God may even expand our theologies. Susan's verbatim in chapter 1 offers such possibilities. Susan's God reveals herself as a numinous female figure that embraces her in a loving and tender way. Her director's theological background could have compelled Susan to dismiss this image of the feminine in God as impossible or as something to be discouraged. The director's theological perspective could have limited her ability to receive Susan's experience and attentively notice how God was choosing to reveal God's self to her. The director could have tried to refocus Susan on the "face of Christ," with which she was praying, thus discouraging this emergence of feminine images and qualities in God. Susan's director, however, was fully aware of theological developments in feminist theology as well as feminine images of God in the women's mystical tradition. Her director was acutely interested in how these images and this theology emerged spontaneously in Susan's prayer within the spiritual direction session. Susan benefited from her director's theological background as a resource.

If our theologies are too narrow, we may focus our attention and our exploration around only one or two kinds of experiences of grace and as a result miss all the rest. If our theologies are too rigid, we may decide that God cannot surprise either our directees or ourselves with new experiences of grace. Those of us who have learned to focus on what we commonly call "religious experience" may be sensitive to the dramatic and palpable manifestations of grace but may overlook more "ordinary" experiences. We develop habits of listening to the unmistakable events, like Saul being knocked from his horse by lightening, but may miss the more subtle moments in which God can only clearly be recognized in retrospect.[3] Our directees may even neglect to mention these latter experiences because they are not sure anything happened. A sense of the horizon of faith in which spiritual direction takes place as well as an adequate theology of grace and of the Holy Spirit prove extremely helpful to spiritual directors as they listen to their directee's narratives.

As directees grow and mature in the spiritual life, directors should begin to see a unique and original appropriation of the mysteries of Christian faith in each. It is reasonable to expect that people whose spiritual lives take place within the context of Christian faith communities will change, personalize, and grow in their theological understandings and articulation of their faith. They will discover these mysteries coming alive within their own experience[4] and frequently turn to scriptural or theological language and themes to express them.

A directee named William offers just such an example. Here he reflects theologically on his experience of receiving the grace of forgiveness, interpreting it as one result of a larger transformation from self-centeredness to God-centeredness.

> There was a time when I had a terrible ego problem. It was all me, me, me, me, and in the last fifteen years, I've learned that the me, the ego, is…something to be ignored, putting one's personality aside and thinking of the other's needs. I used to think of my own needs first and I thought I was being holy at the time, so now I place my ego as much as I can to the side, always saying [to Jesus], "What do you need? What do you want? What would you do?" Through this gift, I've been able to go to people that really hurt one of my daughters. My wife still wouldn't talk to them but when someone was dying in their family, I went to my enemies and I knocked on the door and I said, look, I'm a eucharistic minister and I know your father is dying. Would you like me to bring communion? Well, they broke down and so did I. And then the mother-in-law died and I brought communion again, so I became a sacramental minister to people that injured my family. It was a beautiful gift, but if my old ego had been in place, my pride would have [gotten in the way], and I would have been unforgiving, which is stupid. I wouldn't have been charitable and I would have been condemning myself because we are going to be forgiven as…as we forgive. So when the whole thing was over, I said, "Oh my

God, you gave me this gift to forgive people that were so inju-
rious to my family. You helped me to forgive them." Now if terrible me can forgive, how much more will my God be able to
forgive me. Now I wasn't in it for a trade-off, you know.[5]

This entire passage shows the process of theological reflection spontaneously emerging. William recognizes that he has,
over the last fifteen years, gradually become less self-centered
through the ongoing grace of Christ. He realizes that this was
not something he himself could bring about and turns to Jesus in
his prayer, asking for guidance: "What do you need? What do
you want? What would you do?" When confronted with the
needs of his enemies, he discovered the answers to those questions arising in his behavior. He felt Jesus wanted him to offer
sacramental ministry to a family who had injured his own.

Notice how William reflects theologically on his experience afterwards. He recognizes that he could never have
knocked on his neighbor's door with an offer of communion in
his former ego state. He expresses awe and gratitude at what
God has done in him. He realizes he has received the gift of forgiveness. Even more than that, he reflects on who he discovers
God is. If William, self-centered as he feels himself to be, can
forgive an injury, how much more so does God? William's way
of thinking about God seems to have changed. When he says,
"…I wasn't in it for a trade-off, you know," he suggests that he
didn't forgive his neighbors *because* that was a condition for
God's forgiveness. He forgave his neighbors because God
enabled that forgiveness, and as a result William understands
God's goodness.

Among recently trained spiritual directors, few may be
skilled in responding to the theological dimension of William's
experience. Influenced by a therapeutic emphasis, these directors may dismiss their directees' attempts to relate their faith
experience to their faith tradition. They may listen instead with

a primarily therapeutic concern for negative emotions and unconscious conflicts. By failing to recognize this meaning-making activity of faith as an important aspect of spiritual development, these directors may become bored or uneasy with their directees' theological descriptions. The experience of spiritual direction is the poorer for it. Some directors are so uncomfortable when directees theologize from their religiously significant experiences that they accuse them of "intellectualizing," instead of appreciating their directees' deepening, experiential appropriation of one of the great Christian mysteries. There is a place for thinking about the faith in Christian life—and frequently, that thinking leads to experienced mysteries.

According to storyteller-theologian John Shea, religious traditions provide believers with a common language, symbols, and rituals, which help us interpret our experience.[6] Some of us have problems with theological concepts, however, because they come before we have any experience through which to grasp them. William, for example, knew Christians ought to forgive their enemies. He also knew what it felt like to be unable to do so, a feeling his wife was still experiencing. When it came, the grace of forgiveness felt indescribably different than he expected. And yet he realized the mystery of forgiveness had come alive in him.

Spiritual directors who do not expect directees to describe experiences and formulate personal faith interpretations may either be oblivious to this dimension of spiritual direction or feel a need to control their directees' interpretations with their own theological understandings and language. Neither response is particularly helpful to directees, and both overlook an important aspect of spiritual direction. It is important to pay attention to the theological interpretations of our directees' experiences as they emerge in their narratives and are explicitly expressed in their explanations. This noticing and theologizing is best done within the directees' worldviews and in relationship to aspects of interpretation that will foster the directees' ongoing response to God and the mystery they are encountering.

This is, of course, only one aspect of the conversation. But experiences not interpreted in relationship to Christian faith are not fully appropriated. They can remain so inchoate that a mystical deepening of the directee in the theological direction suggested by the experience may not occur. William did his own subsequent interpretation, which led to a second religious experience of God's willingness and ability to forgive. Had William focused exclusively on his empowered forgiving, his director might have asked what, if anything, his experience might have shown him about God.

Experiences of Spirit

William's case leads us into our exploration of experiences of Spirit. His description exemplifies both dramatic and obvious experiences of grace as well as very subtle ones that require subsequent reflection to fully appropriate them. Spiritual directors need to be able to find both kinds of "gold" in their directees' narratives. William's grace-empowered ability to forgive his enemy was so dramatic he could not miss it. It stood out in his experience. But the more subtle flecks of gold appearing over fifteen years that worked away at his self-centeredness required greater scrutiny, more active searching among all the "stuff" that constituted his stream of life.

This section describes a wide range of experiences of the Spirit in order to give a sense of what they feel like embedded in people's concrete narratives. In these reflections, I am following Karl Rahner's theology of grace, the experience of the Spirit. Rahner speaks eloquently, even poetically, about experiences of God that occur in our everyday life. He insisted that grace is, in fact, experienced.[7] He argued against a purely meta-physical description of grace in which the subject was ontologically changed by grace, changed in the structure of one's being, but could not discover grace operative in any part of actual experience. For Rahner, the "essence of grace [is] the self-communication of God to the transcendent spirit of [men and women]."[8] This experience of God's self-communication has the effect of transforming and ordering persons toward God in knowledge and in love. Thus, grace divinizes persons by making this movement toward God and participation in God possible.

The understanding that Christianity itself is based on the actual experience of the community of believers has caused a shift in theology during recent years. If there were no experiences of the risen Jesus, we would not be here as a gathered community of Christians. As a result, theologians and writers such as Karl Rahner, Edward Schillebeeckx, Frederick Buechner, Monika Hellwig, Elizabeth Johnson, and Elizabeth Dryer, among others, relate their theological reflection to actual experience, either historical or contemporary. The most helpful theology for living the faith or assisting the process of spiritual direction is not detached, abstract intellectualizing, but truthful and illuminating reflection on human experience touched by grace.

Positive Experiences

In his brief essay "Experiencing the Spirit," Karl Rahner describes two distinct types of experiences. Positive experiences are moments in which a sacramental sensibility seems to overtake us, so that God's presence, light, love, and glory shine through them. These occur in our conscious awareness when another's love dissolves us in awe at God's love for us, or we experience unexpected moments of surpassing beauty, or have a sense of the sheer mystery of every created thing from the intricacy of the cosmos to the mystery of every human being, or fill with sheer joy at our cocreativity with God experienced in the birth of a child.[9]

I characterize this first type as experiences of light, love, joy, wonder, or gratitude. This is also the worldview Annie Dillard so eloquently evokes in *Pilgrim at Tinker Creek* and other writings.[10] For her, the universe is literally filled with treasures, and she helps us see and experience the world more wondrously and transparently than we might without her. Frequently, these are experiences of nature or experiences of love and affection that make us feel both worthy and blessed. They tend to support an attitude of trust toward life and fill us with awe and gratitude. In such experiences we feel ourselves addressed by another, somehow drawn outside of or beyond ourselves. They draw us to contemplation——an appreciative, "long, loving look at the real," to use theologian Walter Burghardt's phrase. Some people literally live in such a transfigured universe much of the time and have many such experiences.

Negative Experiences

Because I think most spiritual directors are more attuned to recognizing these positive experiences, I want to focus our attention a bit more closely on a second category of experiences Rahner develops in this essay. These feel more negative, and he talks about them as experiences of the "cracks" in our interpretations and encounters. He suggests that experiences of the Spirit meet us when "everyday realities break and dissolve"[11]— when things fall apart or when things and people fail us. What then? Is there any light that illumines this kind of darkness? When our world or our relationships, which felt reliable, fall apart, we are thrown back on ourselves. We may feel down, overcome, and especially at such times, moved in some strange way by God's Spirit in us. Here Rahner describes some possibilities:

- ...someone who tries to love God although no response of love seems to come from God's silent inconceivability, although no wave of emotive wonder any longer supports him, although he can no longer confuse himself and his life-force with God; although he thinks he will die from such a love, because it seems like death and absolute denial; because with such a love one appears to call into the void and the completely unheard-of; because this love seems like a ghastly leap into groundless space; because everything seems untenable and apparently meaningless.[12]
- [A woman] who discovers that she can forgive though she receives no reward for it, and silent forgiveness from the other side is taken as self-evident.
- [A man] who does his duty where it can apparently only be done with the terrible feeling that he is denying himself and doing something ludicrous for which no one will thank him.
- [A woman] who is really good to someone from whom no echo of understanding and thankfulness is heard in return, whose goodness is not even repaid by the feeling of having been selfless, noble, and so on.
- [A man] who is silent, although he could defend himself, although he is unjustly treated, who keeps silence without feeling that his silence is his sovereign unimpeachability.
- [A woman] who suddenly notices how the tiny trickle of her life wanders through the wilderness of the banality of existence, apparently without aim and with the heartfelt fear of complete exhaustion. And yet she

hopes, she knows not how, that this trickle will find the infinite expanse of the ocean, even though it may still be covered by the grey sands which seem to extend for ever before her.

Rahner expands these examples with another set of experiences, which are given below. These share a hope beyond individual hopes, a basic and fundamental faith that cannot be shaken, although there appears to be no warrant for it. Such hope emerges precisely in the midst of opposition, when things do not seem to be going as we want them to. We live in a culture that often suggests the universe is entirely benign. If we are not receiving its good gifts, we must be looking in the wrong place. In this context, how can we account for that leap of faith, hope, and love that arises in us when there is apparently no justification for it? Where does that come from? Rahner would say it is the action of the Spirit in us. For instance:

- where a responsibility in freedom is still accepted and borne where it has no apparent offer of success and advantage;
- where a man experiences and accepts his ultimate freedom which no earthly compulsions can take away from him;
- where the leap into the darkness of death is accepted as the beginning of everlasting promise;
- where the sum of all accounts of life, which no one can calculate alone, is understood by an inconceivable other as good, though it still cannot be "proven";
- where the fragmentary experience of love, beauty, and joy is experienced and accepted purely and simply as the promise of love, beauty, and joy, without being understood in ultimate cynical scepticism as a cheap form of consolation for some final deception;

- where [a woman] dares to pray into a silent darkness and knows that she is heard, although no answer seems to come back about which she might argue and rationalize;
- where [men or women] rehearse their own deaths in everyday life, and try to live in such a way as they would like to die, peaceful and composed...

—*there* is God and God's liberating grace.[13]

In each of the above examples, Rahner illustrates the texture of transcendental experiences in everyday life. These experiences cannot be accounted for by natural goodness, optimism, or kindness. Rather, they disclose within themselves the Holy Mystery, who makes our very being possible and from whom these responses originate. Thus, they liberate us from self-centeredness, revealing how we already lean toward God even though that is not thematically named. To use theological categories, they are manifestations of the theological virtues of faith, hope, and love emerging in a grace-empowered way in a person's experience rather than through the force of will.

Clearly experiences of faith in action, they capture the way we or our directees simply live our lives rather than religious experiences we might report. In spiritual direction sessions, I hear stories of the most uncommon fidelity and generosity in loving other people. Yet these directees often feel they're barely getting by. The challenges in their lives, which make these choices difficult to sustain, rob them of the awareness of their constancy. Yet they get up every day and love the same people, considering it simply the human thing to do. It is important for us as directors to reflect back to our directees how we see them incarnating Jesus for us. We need to name for them the Jesus kind of behavior they may not recognize in themselves.

Signs of Liberating Grace

Drawing on the work of theologian Edward Schillebeeckx, Elizabeth Dreyer offers a similar set of qualities that point to experiences of grace as liberation. If these dispositions spontaneously emerge in our directees' narratives, we can, once we explore the situations in which they occur, point to the signs of liberating grace we hear. We can ask questions such as: "Is this response coming from your willful determination or from somewhere else?" "Is it your natural optimism?" "Have you always responded this way to this kind of situation?" If these graced responses are mysterious to the directee, we can ask, "What might account for this?" and so begin to appropriate what God might be doing in them. The directee's possible graced responses are included in the following table.

Although these examples may seem a bit abstract, they might serve as a shorthand code of ways we might recognize what God might be "up to." I am beginning to sketch for you a theology of grace. These signs indicate how we and our directees experience ourselves as gifted and graced. Many of the above examples of liberating grace and the experiences of the Spirit that emerge in the "cracks" of our lives reveal to us that God is indeed active. We realize this precisely because we know that we are incapable of responding with faith, hope, and love unless enabled by grace. From Rahner's perspective, these difficult experiences are more easily distinguished from ordinary, natural goodness. In most experiences of this sort, there is no extrinsic reward, not even the affirmation of feeling good about ourselves.

Because of our contemporary awareness of codependent behavior, careful discernment is required to distinguish between compulsive rather than free responses of faith, hope, and love in such difficult circumstances. We may be tempted to caution our directees that their love and constancy is code-

Directee's responses

Freedom for:

freedom
righteousness
peace with God/others
confidence in life
new creation
restoration of all things
joy
happiness
living
life in eternal glory
love
hope
sanctification
ethical commitment to the good
all that is true, noble,
    just, pure, attractive,
    deserving of love
to be generous and warm
    to each other
to overcome evil with good
to share goods
    for healing
    and making whole
to be imitators of God
to walk in love
    as Christ loved us.

Freedom from:

sin
guilt
existential anxieties
    fear of demons
    the grip of fate
    death
    everyday cares/concerns
    sorrow
    despair/hopelessness
dissatisfaction with
    God/others
no freedom
oppressive/alienating ties
lovelessness
arbitrariness
egotism
exploitation of credibility
merciless condemnation of
    others
concern about reputation
trying to impress others
panic
absence of pleasure[14]

pendent behavior instead of potentially an experience of the liberating power of Jesus. A codependent narrative will characteristically lack freedom, while grace-empowered loving will exhibit considerable interior freedom, even though a directee may describe it as a necessary way of behaving. This kind of grace, nevertheless, will not "feel" good because of the degree of suffering present. In our present cultural context, acting from such interior conviction has become suspect even in religious traditions that foster self-giving love.

Hopefully, these descriptive signs of liberating grace and experiences of the Spirit, which are based on the work of Karl Rahner and Edward Schillebeeckx, bring to mind similar experiences. William's case illustrated the way one directee noticed and reflected on the effects of grace in his life. He was conscious of receiving the grace of forgiveness and recognized that no one else in his family had been empowered with forgiving and forbearing love toward the family that had injured his. When he reached out to his enemies as a ministering member of the larger community, William discovered that God had given him the grace to talk with the family. Later, as he assimilated this experience, the mystery of God as forgiver and of God's action in his life reverberated in his consciousness. He turned immediately to the forgiving God revealed to him through his own grace-empowered ability to forgive.

The following narrative is somewhat more opaque. Judy, a thirty-eight-year-old woman, poignantly describes surviving her family as an experience of grace in her life. Her narrative sparkles with small flecks of the gold of emerging freedom and hints of liberating grace:

> Just the fact that I LIVED through my family experience all in one piece, mentally—most days! And that I'm functional. Well one of the twelve steps is: "Turn our lives and our wills over to the care of God, as we understand God." And...ever since I've

done THAT, and I did that in the presence of a sponsor, because I worked at steps one through nine on the emotional incest issues. I'd done enough in therapy on those issues, and she recommended I do this, and...it was the best advice she ever gave me! It's just been a real difference since I've done that. That was...two years ago. There's a real sense that, even though I may get frustrated, there's a REAL...there's a back-drop. It's like, on a stage. It's the backdrop of..."it really is going to be OK." I mean, there will be days when I scream and yell, and all this. But there really is a sense in my life that I AM going to get taken care of, that I am going to survive, that I am going to flourish. That God wants all that for me. Not that my life will be without pain, and boredom, and other things, but that God really, really wants the very best for me, and that if we work in partnership together, then I can allow (laughs) that to happen! And ALLOW good things to come into my life! And so, it has changed my ordinary life, in the sense that it has just...calmed me down. I don't get hysterical about things I have no control over. I mean, I really do live one day at a time; I spent eight months being in this career transition, and just realizing that now, whatever is going to happen is going to happen, and that I need to turn things over to God, and that there's a mystery to life. Before, I used to sit down and try to figure it out and solve it. I realize there are several right choices here, probably, and that there are shades of grey, and that if I'm open to what God—even if I screw up—God is going to eventually get me on track. And it's a sense of...that I'm being carried on a wave.[15]

This is the narrative of a person in recovery. It clearly illustrates the sense of freedom emerging in Judy's experience, which she describes as "being carried on a wave." She identi-fies this "wave" with God's presence in her life and its effect on her. She is at an earlier stage in the spiritual life, one in which she struggles to surrender herself to God and to trust that God will treat her differently than her family did. Her operative theology supports this effort because she has "a sense...that I *AM* going to get taken care of, that I am going to survive, that I am going to flourish. That God wants all that for me."

Both examples illustrate the gradual process of recognizing grace through subsequent reflection. William describes an experience in which the ability to forgive and to reconcile happened in him. After the experience, the grace deepens as he realizes both the way God has enabled this forgiveness and how God forgives. For Judy, who grew up in a very abusive family, the emergence of peacefulness and freedom and growing trust signals empowering grace. This change occurs through the combination of adult children of alcoholics–oriented therapy and her experience of God. She can describe the difference between compulsive, unfree behavior and the emergence of a reliable sense of being cared for. She can distinguish her unique form of liberating grace when something from beyond herself operates in and through her and she no longer controls everything. In these two examples, subsequent reflection within the spiritual direction context helped the directees name and reexperience liberating grace with deeper appropriation.

In the research from which I selected these descriptive narratives,[16] I found the need for time, introspection, and subsequent reflection very common. When life events or persons mediated the experience of God, only one-third of the people interviewed could identify those experiences in subsequent reflection. Half of the people interviewed were aware immediately of something mysterious and unnamable at work in the experience, but they also required subsequent reflection to grasp it more thoroughly. For the remainder, whose experiences were more immediately transparent to the Mystery, reflecting on the experience theologically deepened it further. This highlights something we as spiritual directors most likely already know— our directees only recognize a small fraction of their actual experiences of grace without the facilitation of spiritual direction.

The entire first group mentioned above would most likely fail to uncover their stories of faith were they not in spiritual direction. This seems especially true for those whose experiences do not take place during times of solitude, liturgy, or prayer. The clues identified by an experiential theology of grace guide our exploration and reflection with these directees. Further bits of gold may then appear in their stream of life as a result of exploring these moments of grace more deeply. In spiritual direction, there are always two sides to this: What is God up to? and How is the directee responding? Sometimes we catch the God part of the story, but sometimes we can only infer God's action from directees' accounts of their inexplicable responses to something not quite fully grasped.

Mysteries of Faith

The remainder of this chapter explores directees' explicit experience of and response to one of the mysteries of faith. These mysteries are the traditional ways the churches theologically symbolize the triune God and Christian life lived in relationship to the God revealed in Jesus. One can think about this by recalling the various portions of the ancient creeds and other core themes, such as those listed in the following table, used in liturgical or catechetical contexts.

From the earliest times, these brief formulas were understood as symbols pointing toward the mystery of life as experienced in Christ. Symbols point toward the inexhaustible mysteries of faith. As directors, we might treat these words (now theological categories) as symbols—pointers toward a reality that explodes beyond containment by words and definitions. This doctrinal shaping of Christian experience is rooted in, and presumes, the more ample narratives and teachings in the Scriptures. Together the symbols of the creed and the "Good

Mysteries of Christian Faith

Trinity
God/Holy Mystery
Source/Unoriginate/Abba/Father
Son/Word/Jesus/Savior
    Creation
    Incarnation
    Kingdom of God
    Suffering Witness
    Redemption/Salvation/Healing
    Death
    Resurrection of Jesus
Holy Spirit
Vocation/Call/Discipleship
Church/Body of Christ/People of God/*Koinonia*
Diakonia/Service
Communion of Saints/Communion in Holy Things
Mary
Disciple/Follower/Lover/Friend/Beloved/Faithful
Sacraments/Cosmos/Eucharist
Baptism/Confirmation/Anointing of the Sick
Healing/Forgiveness/Reconciliation
Marriage/Ordination
Eschatology
    Death
    Heaven, Hell, Purgatory
    Resurrection of the Body
    Life Everlasting
Will of God
Agape/Love (*Koinonia*, Friends, Strangers, Enemies)
Beatitudes
Spiritual and Corporal Works of Mercy
Grace
Deification/Divinization (*Theosis*)
Providence
Revelation/Inspiration/Illumination
Angels
Demons

News" of God's involvement with us contribute toward the shaping of that same experience, giving us rich and multiple metaphors for the life we share in Christ.

Contemporary theological reflection in all but the fundamentalist traditions understands that our theological language contributes to the shaping of our experience. None has any "raw" experience; our experience is always interpreted through the frames of reference we already have. Sometimes we may need to take a vacation from doctrinal words because they have lost meaning for us. Eventually, though, if we are to appropriate our mystical experience—our deep experiences of God—in the context of Christian faith and tradition, we need to relocate it within the horizon of faith revealed in Jesus.

It makes a difference whether or not we name something within Christian tradition. When we personally recognize that an experience of God in prayer is an experience of, for instance, God as Trinity, our appreciation of that mystery deepens. It becomes real for us in more than a notional way. Our experience leads us to wonder and contemplate what this particular mystery might have been for others in the tradition. We discover that we have not only received a tradition of faith, but also participate in it and contribute to it as well. We begin to believe on the basis of something we have experienced as well as on the basis of the witness of others.

In *Uncovering Stories of Faith* I described how the stories of grace that directees share in spiritual direction already constitute an interpretation. A particular theology is already embedded in the narrative of our experiences, and so we do well to pay attention to the theological worldview within which our directees interpret their experience. When directors help their directees notice the encounter with the mysteries of faith as part of the ongoing process of revelation, directees begin to feel more connected to their own religious tradition. They begin to understand that Christian faith and theology is expansive enough to encompass the multiple shifts of accumulated meaning that result from their lived experience of the Spirit here and now.

Whenever "new experience" contradicts a received theology or different people in the Christian community begin to participate in theological reflection, new theological insights emerge.[17] We no longer believe in the same way because we have been changed by our experiences; we seek to understand from this new perspective.[18] Many people who engage in spiritual direction are going through profound changes in their theological perspectives. For instance, women are attempting to reshape theology from within female experience and in a way that renders them visible and fully participative in the Christian mysteries. Lay men and women are articulating theologies of marriage, friendship, and relationship. Many of us are reinterpreting our operative theologies in relationship to the new cosmology and emerging story of the universe, which explains why eschatology is currently becoming a creative area of theological exploration. Some, for example, are exploring how the idea of a "new heaven and new earth" may relate to this world and this earth.

For purposes of illustration, I will discuss only a few contemporary examples of the mysteries of faith, the communion of saints and the will of God, especially as they touch upon suffering and death. New insights about these mysteries are common experiences of our directees today, for both our cultures and our churches are changing in response to major paradigm shifts, especially those from the sciences. Any article of the creed could emerge within our directees' rich experience of Christian life at any time. There is always room for doing theology out of our contemplative experience, and each of us needs to articulate at different times in our lives what we actually believe. Nicholas Lash poetically describes our relationship with the creed we profess in worship and praise as "short words and endless learning."[19] Christian faith is truly a process of endless learning.

The Communion of Saints

As I grow older and as I become more experienced as a spiritual director, I notice that some mysteries of the faith that I espoused but that never really directly affected my life have suddenly become numinous and more significant. Themes relating to the communion of saints, the resurrection of the body, and life everlasting, for example, frequently emerge in middle-aged directees. The experience of bereavement often leads believers to wonder about where their beloved dead are as well as what will happen to them after death.

A member of my religious community first brought this mystery to my attention. She reported having never really understood much about "the communion of saints" until her father, to whom she was very close, died. When she went through the process of grieving his death, she was both surprised and deeply consoled by reflecting upon the meaning of this mystery. The experience of bereavement invites us to search our tradition for whatever symbols and beliefs ease our grief without denying the factual loss. For some, the promise of resurrection helps; for others, the communion of saints; for still others, a conviction about God's love, forgiveness, and compassion. Directees find themselves praying to or continuing to communicate with their beloved dead, sometimes for a while, sometimes for the rest of their lives.

Without having yet buried a parent, I, too, find myself reflecting on and praying into the mystery of the communion of saints. Community members with whom I have lived and who have affected me in many ways are now dying. Many of my friends and acquaintances seem to be confronting the mystery of parents' diminishment, aging, illness, suffering, and death itself. Yet death is integral to life; within the Christian perspective death does not have the last word. Implicit in this mystery is the sense that despite the actual loss of persons as we have known them, there may remain a continued sense of presence to the bereaved and a hope for future reunion.

The death of a parent or another beloved may initiate quite different responses. One directee, Cora, began reading *God's Ecstasy* by Beatrice Bruteau.[20] The deeper she immersed herself in the new story of the universe, a less personal and more cosmic story, the more she began to doubt the possibility of any afterlife. The mysteries of faith that deal with the communion of saints, the resurrection of the body, and life everlasting lost all reality for Cora, and she became frightened when she thought about her father's dying. She continues to work at integrating her new understandings in ways that do not completely deny what she once, albeit perhaps too literally, understood. Cora struggles with this challenge to her faith relationship with God and to the way she has understood that faith.

Ironically, others who read Bruteau's reflection on the communion of saints in *Radical Optimism* found their horizon enlarged, for she evokes the way the saintly dead are present to us in a mystical way just as the divine Persons of the Trinity indwell us. When Bruteau, drawing on the meaning of the Latin word *sancta*, expands this notion to include a communion in holy things as well as persons, the entire cosmos lights up aspects of God's sacramental presence in creation and in the community gathered for sacramental worship. Bruteau is like our directees. She is simply trying to understand, from the perspective of her contemplative experience and new worldview, how she might understand this mystery of faith and what claims this understanding might make on her decisions as well as her consciousness.[21]

This same mystery of the communion of saints need not be entered exclusively through bereavement. The annual liturgical feast day of All Saints invites reflection on all the unnamed, uncanonized "saints" we have known either historically or personally. I was deeply moved at an Easter Vigil service in which I heard Catherine McAuley, the founder of my religious community, honored in the litany of saints, along with Oscar Romero, Dorothy Day, Martin Luther King, and others who were acknowledged as "saints" in this local community. Such naming of people who are saints for a local community lessens the political and doctrinal tensions in the larger church. It is one way that long-standing customs and the resources of Christian tradition invite an empowering and innovating response in faith.

The Will of God

The struggle to understand and respond to the will of God in situations of sin, suffering, and death is another mystery of faith that frequently emerges in the lives of directees. I would like to give you a couple of examples of ordinary believers who theologize freshly on the "will of God," a theological symbol that admits of both liberating and oppressive interpretations. Too often, the will of God has been used to maintain situations of oppression rather than mobilize resistance to conditions that are the result of sin and not God's will. Experiences of the Spirit liberate, not oppress. Even when experiences of the Spirit lead us to suffering and death, they are not oppressive, for they energize us with hope beyond the present situation. They support our humanity and personhood, and they expand our reality, not contract it.

An example of a liberating understanding of the will of God in a situation of suffering and death comes from a former graduate student. Theresa, a married lay missionary, shared this experience from her pastoral work in Peru.

> My greatest teachers about the will of God were the women I encountered on the outskirts of Lima, Peru. Their context was urban poverty; their lives much sinned against. When their

children died, and many children died, it was often called either God's will or God's punishment. One night we reflected on that reality in the family catechetical program. The discussion began to focus on how God's will is not that people be oppressed. Everything we see through Jesus is the proclamation of life and abundance. So it was that the mothers concluded that their children's deaths were the will, not of God, but of bad water. A great deal of what happens in human life is contrary to the will of God. What God wills and calls us to is continual emergence from the tomb. To translate these lessons from Lima to my own life continues to be a process of conversion. It is the will of God that I engage in that process, name the bad water in my life for what it is and through my actions find a new, life-giving well.[22]

This brief example offers a flavor of the kind of "grass-roots" theological reflection done by ardent believers who are trying to make sense of painful, challenging experiences in a way that does not destroy belief and trust in a benevolent, wholeness-making God. They resist turning God into a malevolent being that relishes our suffering while at the same time resisting the urge to deny the pain and anguish of the situation.

I have walked with directees and friends whose entire faith life seemed to collapse under the weight of watching a loved family member or friend suffer in seemingly needless ways. Confrontation with the mystery of evil, suffering, and death pushes us into new understandings. Our formulations are neither entirely orthodox nor even entirely adequate, but this witness from a base community of women in Lima gave me hope and lived on in Theresa's life. The metaphor of "bad water" works both emotionally and theologically in such a way that hope is nurtured and endurance of suffering sustained because these children died from most likely avoidable causes.

Frederick Buechner offers another reflection on the will of God in *Telling Secrets*. Using biblical symbols, he struggles to come to terms with his father's suicide many years after the fact.

The God of biblical faith is a God who started history going in the first place. He is also a God who moment by moment, day by day continues to act in history always, which means both the history that gets written down in the *New York Times* and the *San Francisco Chronicle* and at the same time my history and your history, which for the most part don't get written down anywhere except in the few lines that may be allotted to us some day on the obituary page. The Exodus, the Covenant, the entry into the Promised Land—such mighty acts of God as these appear in Scripture, but no less mighty are the acts of God as they appear in our own lives. I think of my father's death as in its way his exodus, his escape from bondage, and of the covenant that my mother made with my brother and me never to talk about him, and of the promised land of pre-World War II Bermuda that we reached through the wilderness and bewilderness of our first shock and grief at losing him.

As I understand it, to say that God is mightily present even in such private events as these does not mean that he makes events happen to us which move us in certain directions like chessmen. Instead, events happen under their own steam as random as rain, which means that God is present in them not as their cause but as the one who even in the hardest and most hair-raising of them offers us the possibility of that new life and healing which I believe is what salvation is. For instance I cannot believe that a God of love and mercy in any sense willed my father's suicide; it was my father himself who willed it as the only way out available to him from a life that for various reasons he had come to find unbearable. God did not will what happened that early November morning in Essex Fells, New Jersey, but I believe that God was present with my father—I can guess how he was present with my father—I can guess much better how utterly abandoned by God my father must have felt if he thought about God at all—but my faith as well as my prayer is that he was and continues to be present with him in ways beyond my guessing. I can speak with some assurance only of how God was present in that dark time for me in the sense that I was not destroyed by it but came out of it with scars that I bear to this day, to be sure, but also somehow the wiser and the stronger for it. Who knows how I might have turned out if my father had lived, but through the loss of him all those years ago I think that I learned something about how even tragedy can be a means of grace that I might never come to any other way. As I see it, in other words, God acts in history and in your and my brief histories not as the puppeteer who sets the scene and works the strings but rather as the great director who no matter what role fate casts us in conveys to us somehow from the wings, if we have our eyes, ears, hearts open and sometimes even if we don't, how we can play those roles in a way to enrich and ennoble and hallow the whole vast drama of things including our own small but crucial parts in it.[23]

These are just two examples of how different believers, under the sway of the Spirit, have come to understand some very difficult experiences in ways that keep them in relationship with a loving Mystery and bring hope and life and healing. For Buechner, daring to tell the story of his father's death finally freed him from the burden of this secret. Eventually, he could no longer avoid the struggle to find some theological resolution to this painful experience.

We and our directees can discover that by discerning where and how we experience God in such difficult situations and by simultaneously struggling to rearticulate it for ourselves contributes greatly to a positive faith-filled outcome. This will not happen instantly. The examples above were written years after a resolution had occurred. That differs greatly from a directee opening to the revealing mystery of God in the midst of such difficult experiences. Nevertheless, it is important to listen to how directees make sense of such experience in faith and to support them in the struggle. Frequently, if we engage it and patiently allow it to unfold, unbelief or changed belief leads to a more adult, more mature faith perspective, as these latter two incidents illustrate.

As spiritual directors, we need to be careful not to impose our theological resolutions or positions on our directees. When directees describe a theological approach very different from our own, we may need to work with our affective responses so they do not get in the way of directees' meaning-making process. We need to pay attention in supervision to theological conflicts of interpretation as well as our counter-transference reactions. By reflecting on our strong reactions, we learn ways to plant seeds and open possibilities to our directees without imposing our own views. The women of Lima found their own theological resolution in their community of faith. So, too, will our directees.

Theological Issues in the Ignatian Retreat

Up to this point, this chapter has primarily focused on the theological dimension of spiritual direction specifically within the context of ongoing spiritual direction rather than direction given during retreats. Spiritual directors familiar with the *Spiritual Exercises* of St. Ignatius recognize that this personal appropriation of the mysteries of faith is not only one of the explicit graces sought in the retreat, but also a means of facilitating conversion in the directee. Such was the experience of Ignatius himself on the banks of the Cardoner River:

> While he was seated there, the eyes of his understanding
> began to be opened; not that he saw any vision, but he under-
> stood and learnt many things, both spiritual matters and mat-
> ters of faith and scholarship, and this with so great an
> enlightenment that everything seemed new to him.
>
> This left his understanding so enlightened that he felt as if he
> were another man with another mind.[24]

Harvey Egan believes this experience may have provided the inspiration for the "Principle and Foundation" consideration that begins the *Exercises* and suggests, "Ignatius received a mystically infused sense of the unity of the Christian mysteries."[25] He thus wanted others to understand and respond to the Christian mysteries—creation, Trinity, incarnation, redemption, salvation—through an intimate experience of the Persons of the Trinity and the intentions and desires of this triune God toward the world.

Because these mysteries weave through the entire retreat, many Ignatian-trained directors may either unconsciously impose on directees the historical theological horizon of Ignatius's own times or assume the theological dimension is inconsequential. A number of contemporary commentators on the *Exercises* have explicitly dealt with reinterpreting and updating the *Exercises* within an adequate theological view.[26]

When spiritual direction takes place within a context other than the *Spiritual Exercises* of St. Ignatius, the mysteries of Christian faith may emerge as a response to the liturgical year, meditation on Scripture, or the challenge of life events. Directees in the context of ongoing spiritual direction or a time of retreat not structured by the *Exercises* are not "programmed" to encounter these mysteries in any particular sequence, as happens in the *Exercises*. As a consequence, directors need to be even more attentive in order to identify the mysteries of faith emerging in this less predictable way.

Responses to Theological Content

In the spiritual direction conversation, we can interact with the theological dimension in a number of ways. In the first part of the chapter, I encourage directors to expand our understandings of what counts as religious experience. I suggest that we follow the clues to depth experiences—the traces of the Spirit we find strewn throughout the stream of life. Where do we experience our directees' courage, selflessness, and faith in their stories? Where do we see their love shown more in deeds than in feelings? In what circumstances do we witness in their sheer tenacity and capacity for endurance? By what do we find them energized and sustained without burning out? If we notice these traces of the Spirit, our directees will begin to appropriate these experiences, too. If their sensitivity to the Spirit's action in their lives increases, their unique world of grace will deepen and become more available in their conscious experience. Any theological naming best occurs at the end of the exploration process. If our directees use a theological word-symbol, we would first explore the experience that initiated their use of the term and then try to discover what new meaning that symbol seems to be gathering for them in the light of the experience they have described.

In our own lives and in those of our directees, the mysteries of faith as articulated in the creed or in the Scriptures occur randomly and piecemeal. It might be possible for some directors to use a simple listing of the mysteries of faith, such as the one above, as a way of preparing themselves to notice how or under what circumstances these mysteries manifest themselves in the ordinary lives of their directees.

Often we are pressed to understand a mystery freshly when it emerges for us in a prayer experience in relationship to a scriptural text or a liturgical event. For example, when we are present at Eucharist and what is signified *happens* in some mysterious way, we wonder about it. When a mystery is tasted, felt, savored, and experienced, it accumulates meaning and evokes response. Who is the Body of Christ? What happens to us as believers when the Body of Christ moves outside of the church and we experience ourselves as one body with the homeless person on the steps? What happens when we recognize a beggar's face as the one face of Christ?

In this chapter, I advocate appropriate ways to pay attention to theological themes in the spiritual direction conversation.[27] Faith *does* seek understanding. Sometimes we may simply connect the directees' richly concrete descriptions with Christian mysteries they may not have named explicitly. A comment, such as "The way you describe this particular experience suggests you might be beginning to experience…in a new way. Does that fit for you? Or would you connect this experience more with some other symbol or mystery?" invites directees' exploration, leaving the interpretation open and tentative.

Sometimes our theological resources are inadequate to our experience and trap us in an inauthentic, immature, and oppressive relationship with God. This also happens to our directees. Knowledge liberates. A fresh theological insight may release a new way God can be God for us and for them. As directors, we need to help our directees identify their constricting, often implicit, theological assumptions and suggest alternative possibilities they might consider. We might do this by offering some spiritual reading that addresses a particular issue. Sometimes directees ask us directly for theological resources. Perhaps we want to be more indirect by raising questions about whether their voiced theology squares with their experience of God over many seasons. Sometimes we might want to help directees find some community context that will support them in the struggle to find their way to new understandings. We may simply want to express gratitude for the way their faith-filled understanding of the mysteries consoles us. Always we will want to stay close to our directees' own language.

As directors, I think we can expect to hear theological themes in the conversation if we listen for them. Often this "grass-roots" theologizing is quite implicit and scarcely noticed by directees themselves. Simply reflecting back what we hear, especially if it feels and sounds true to us, can be deeply reassuring to the directee. Mature mystical development takes directees, and ourselves for that matter, deeper and deeper into the life of God. New facets of the mystery of God open for us. God indwells us, gifts us with the Spirit, and manifests love to the world in and through us. When we live in this climate, we become, as John of the Cross phrased it, "God by participation." Our lives, of course, do not unfold like a theology textbook, but our vibrant, organic Christian lives will eventually personalize the Christian mysteries. As we mature, these mysteries become real to us precisely because they are no longer merely articles in a creed from some earlier time, but because God's animating Spirit gifts us with the same mysteries in our times and in the uniqueness of our own circumstances.

- When or how do you recognize the theological content in your directees' narratives?
- Do experiences come to mind that neither you nor your directees have named as grace? Does it feel right to name them that way now?

- Does your faith community have other words that point to these same kinds of experiences?
- Where do you experience your directees' grace-empowered courage and selflessness in the stories they tell?

NOTES

1. See my *Uncovering Stories of Faith* (Mahwah, N.J.: Paulist Press, 1989), 64–65.

2. See Patricia O'Connell Killen, "Assisting Adults to Think Theologically," in *Method in Ministry: Theological Reflection and Christian Ministry*, rev. ed., ed. James D. and Evelyn E. Whitehead (Kansas City: Sheed & Ward, 1995), 103–11, for a similar form of theological reflection, which usually takes place in a group context.

3. William Barry and William Connolly, through their work at the Center for Religious Development and their book, *The Practice of Spiritual Direction* (New York: Seabury, 1982), greatly assisted spiritual directors in listening for and responding to the religious experiences already transpiring in the directees' lives. The helpful shift to experience caused some directors to neglect other dimensions of the conversation, however.

4. Kathleen Norris has done us all a great service in *Amazing Grace: A Vocabulary of Faith* (New York: Riverhead Books, 1998), where she struggles with the received vocabulary of Christian tradition, infusing these words with meanings that she can relate to and that come from her own gradual experience of coming to belief in adulthood. These reflective essays are literary gems, which resemble the way directees articulate their experiences of faith in more fragmentary and less literary expressions.

5. From interviews conducted in 1990, this particular one conducted with a sixty-eight-year-old married man.

6. See John Shea, *Stories of Faith* (Chicago: Thomas More Press, 1980), 76–125, and *Experiences of the Spirit* (Chicago: Thomas More Press, 1983).

7. In *The Human Experience of God* (Mahwah, N.J.: Paulist Press, 1983), Denis Edwards "translates" this primarily Rahnerian perspective in a helpful and accessible manner.

8. Karl Rahner, "Enthusiasm and Grace" in *Theological Investigations: Experience of the Spirit*, vol. 16, trans. David Morland (New York: Crossroad, 1983), 40.

9. Karl Rahner, *The Practice of the Faith: A Handbook of Contemporary Spirituality*, ed. Karl Lehmann and Albert Raffelt, trans. John Griffiths (New York: Crossroad, 1986), 80–81.

10. Annie Dillard, *Pilgrim at Tinker Creek* (New York: Bantam, 1975).

11. Rahner, *The Practice of Faith*, 81.

12. Ibid., 82–83. This example and those that follow are taken from this essay and rendered in inclusive language. See also Karl Rahner, "Reflections on the Experience of Grace" in *Theological Investigations: The Theology of the Spiritual Life*, vol. 3, trans. Karl and Boniface Kruger (Baltimore: Helicon Press, 1967), 86–90 for an equally evocative description of experiences of grace.

13. Rahner, *The Practice of Faith*, 83–84. This is an abbreviated list.

14. Elizabeth Dreyer, *Manifestations of Grace* (Wilmington, Del.: Michael Glazier, 1990), 175–76. Dreyer's chart is based on Schillebeeckx's thought.

15. Used with permission of the directee.

16. Janet K. Ruffing, "The World Transfigured: Kataphatic Religious Experience" *Studies in Spirituality* 5 (1995): 241.

17. Hans Georg Gadamer in *Truth and Method*, trans. Garrett Barden and John Cumming (New York: Crossroad, 1975), discusses at length the characteristics of "new experience." He suggests it almost always confounds expectations. Things are not as they might seem to us. This is an existential clue that our interpretative schema may be inadequate to this experience. In this way, new situations, conditions, experiences positively contribute to a received tradition by allowing it to grow.

18. See Berard Marthaler, *The Creed: The Apostolic Faith in Contemporary Theology* (Mystic, Conn.: Twenty-Third Publications,

1993), for descriptions of how the community process of formulating and reformulating the creeds among local churches and later gatherings of bishops is quite similar to the personal process I describe in this section. He also identifies the multiple functions of creeds as: profession of faith, as symbol, as story, as doxology, as rule of faith (see pp. 1–18). Directees or directors, for that matter, who only identify with creedal statements as the rule of faith will be unwilling or even unable to explore theological themes and words as part of an ongoing process of articulating something of the inexhaustible mystery of Christian life. Faith is a process of relationship to the triune God. Relationships change and grow usually through challenge and doubt before they achieve confidence and recommitment.

19. Nicholas Lash, *Believing Three Ways in One God: A Reading of the Apostles' Creed* (Notre Dame: University of Notre Dame Press, 1993), 4. This small, accessible volume, written by a gifted theologian, illuminates the experience of ordinary adult Christians who reflect on their experience through the lens of their faith experience.

20. Beatrice Bruteau, *God's Ecstasy: The Creation of a Self-Creating World* (New York: Crossroad, 1997).

21. Beatrice Bruteau, *Radical Optimism: Rooting Ourselves in Reality* (New York: Crossroad, 1993), 103-16. Some readers may be interested in Elizabeth Johnson's feminist interpretation of the communion of saints in *Friends of God and Prophets: A Feminist Theological Reading of the Communion of Saints* (New York: Crossroad, 1998).

22. See Theresa Rhodes McGee, *The Comforter: Stories of Loss and Rebirth* (New York: Crossroad, 1997), 52–65, for an expanded version of this incident.

23. Frederick Buechner, *Telling Secrets: A Memoir* (San Francisco: Harper, 1993), 30–32.

24. *Ignatius of Loyola: Spiritual Exercises and Selected Writings*, ed. George Ganss, Classics of Western Spirituality (Mahwah, N.J.: Paulist Press, 1991), "The Autobiography," no. 30.

25. Harvey Egan, *Christian Mysticism: The Future of a Tradition* (New York: Pueblo, 1984), 36.

26. See especially, Harvey D. Egan, S.J., *The Spiritual Exercises and the Ignatian Mystical Horizon* (St. Louis, Mo.: Institute for Jesuit

Sources, 1976) and *Christian Mysticism*, 30–79. Others have published theological materials related to interpreting the *Exercises* theologically in *The Way* and *The Supplement to the Way* as well as in *Studies in Jesuit Spirituality* during the last two decades.

27. Some readers may find *The New Dictionary of Catholic Spirituality*, ed. Michael Downey (Collegeville, Minn.: Liturgical Press, 1993) a helpful resource for brief essays related to the spiritual life and contemporary theological reflection in the American Catholic context. Others may find "Living our Theology" in Philip Sheldrake, *Spirituality and Theology: Christian Living and the Doctrine of God* (Maryknoll, N.Y.: Orbis Books, 1998) also helpful.

Chapter 4

SEARCHING FOR THE BELOVED: LOVE MYSTICISM IN SPIRITUAL DIRECTION

Every religious tradition of the world, with perhaps Buddhism as the only exception, fosters some form of love mysticism. As discussed in chapter 1, at the root of all human and divine intimacy is a mutual desiring, regardless of how opaque such desire might be to us. As Christian mystical life progresses, we gradually discover God and ourselves to be in a mutual process. A Sufi aphorism expresses this discovery aptly: "For thirty years I sought God. But when I looked carefully, I saw that in reality God was the Seeker and I was the sought."[1] Love mysticism leads us to God by route of such passionate desire and searching. A second example from Sufism, a story about two human lovers, yields further insight about this process.

> One day Majnun, whose love for Laila inspired many a Persian Poet, was playing in a little heap of sand, when a friend came to him and said: "Why are you wasting your time in an occupation so childish?" "I am seeking Laila in these sands," replied Majnun.

His friend in amazement cried: "Why? Laila is an angel, so what is the use of seeking her in the common earth?" "I seek her everywhere," said Majnun, bowing his head, "that I may find her somewhere."[2]

Laila represents the divine beloved, and Majnun's pursuit, the ransacking of creation for traces of her, exemplifies passionate loving as a way to God. By searching everywhere, the lover discovers that God emerges somewhere in his experience. In and through a created manifestation, the divine beloved makes his or her presence felt, and the lover finds God there. This encounter with the divine may be characterized by feelings of desire, arousal, passion, and union. We often categorize these experiences as mystical, and throughout this chapter these divine-human encounters are referred to as experiences of love mysticism.

There are two different mystical paths that may intertwine. Both require careful discernment in terms of encouraging directees to respond appropriately. One path feels like romantic love: God arouses the desires of the human beloved, engages in courtship, and makes love with the human beloved. The human process of adapting to this reality in the stages of awakening, recognition, purification, surrender, and transformation tend to take place through the alternation of felt presence and absence. This path, which transforms and sublimates passion in ongoing and ever deepening intimacy with God, is the focus in this chapter.

A second path is more apophatic in its feel. It takes place with fewer reported "events." The quality of experience feels more vague. We yearn for God, who paradoxically feels absent and present simultaneously. This path typically minimizes feeling and emphasizes darkness; prayer usually consists of quiet, silent, loving attention toward God.

For both of these paths, and any variations on these themes for individual directees, the dynamics of human-divine intimacy take place on various levels of the existential self. Mystical experiences can affect our superficial, highly conditioned ego awareness, other layers of our psyches, and the core of our souls (or the heart or the true self). Chapter 1, for example, dealt with helping directees recognize and go beyond the wants and desires of the conditioned ego, and chapter 2 focused on unconscious dynamics in the psyche that result in resistance to God's initiatives. The mystical process also affects deeper levels of the psyche, such as in the way some highly numinous dreams reveal God's presence in this part of the self. So, too, visions or words that occur in mystical prayer show effects on the psyche as well as indicating something even deeper going on in the center or the core of the soul.

Ultimately, this core may be experienced in its true condition of being already in union with the divine. The mystical process gradually brings all levels of the self into harmony. Paul writes, "In God, we live, and move, and have our being," and John of the Cross teaches that "God is the center of the soul." Both realized that we are already in God. That we become God not by nature but by participation can only be understood from within the mystical experience itself, beyond the distortions of ego.[3]

Challenges to Spiritual Directors from the Love Mysticism of Directees

Spiritual directors respond to accounts of erotic features in their directees' religious experience with a variety of reactions. Some respond in very helpful ways and others in ways that are problematic. Spiritual directors are not equally competent in companioning directees whose religious experience is characterized by such love mysticism. Since directees them-selves are also frequently ambivalent about these experiences, the discomfort or anxiety of their directors can inhibit or even positively discourage their response to overtures of intimacy initiated by God. When directors encounter this material in their directees' experience, they confront several of the fol-lowing challenges, which touch on deeply personal as well as theoretical issues:

- Spiritual directors frequently become anxious and uncomfortable when directees report intense experi-ences of mystical love, especially if erotic features are disclosed. As a result, they often fail to explore the expe-rience. This reluctance to stay with the experience renders them incapable of noticing where the directee's anxiety may "block" it and close it off before union with God has been reached.
- If spiritual directors are personally unfamiliar with such intimacy with God or are currently grieving the painful absence of such intimacy, they may become envious of their directees. In order to avoid this uncomfortable feel-ing, the director may dismiss the directee's account and neglect to facilitate the directee's deeper exploration of the experience.
- Spiritual directors who do not appreciate the role of desire may fail to explore deeply enough the desires the directee *does* have (for prayer, intimacy with God, or inti-macy with and love for another) and thus miss the oppor-tunity to help the directee become present to his or her own deepest desires.
- Ignatian spiritual directors may not understand how much help directees may actually need in order to "pray for the grace they want." As discussed extensively in chapter 1, directees may not actually know what they

want or may not be prepared to receive the grace they *think* they want, with all of its consequences. Directors can greatly assist directees by helping them clarify illusory from authentic desires.

- Many less experienced spiritual directors are either unfamiliar with the rich traditions of love mysticism in Christian tradition or presume such experiences no longer happen. Directees often share the same assumptions. If they are unfamiliar with the tradition, they may become quite frightened and misinterpret their experience of God as displaced eroticism.[4]

- The progressive, deepening encounter into the mystery of God as the divine beloved, until lover and beloved are experienced as one body and soul, often feels like absence or loss. In actuality, the invitation is to move beyond a subject-object duality. Both directors and directees can misinterpret this subtle unitive movement as an experience of God's absence, because of the change in how God is present to the directee.

- Directors may lack empathy in their responses to directees whose experiences of divine-human love differ from their own. Or directors may be unsupportive of their directees' development because they themselves lack sufficient experience of the mystical. Directors who are unable to achieve empathy toward their directees' mystical experience or who remain unsupportive after seeking competent consultation and supervision may need to refer directees to another spiritual director.

- The vagaries of romantic attachments of all kinds are frequently the opaque manifestations of divine-human intimacy wanting to happen. In so far as spiritual directors feel uncomfortable with or judgmental about their directees' reports of sexual expression, sexual orientations, or romantic attachments, they will not be able to explore the depth of these experiences. This exploration could reveal the soul's searching for its divine beloved and thus facilitate, often with therapeutic help, the harmonizing of these powerful energies in the person.

- Spiritual directors almost always need to explore the relational histories of their directees. Spiritual direction with celibates requires particular attention to their histories of emotional intimacy, friendship, passion, and sexual expression. Spiritual direction with those who are or have been actively involved in sexually expressive relationships also requires an exploration of their relational histories for understanding both the gifts for intimacy and the barriers to it they bring to the divine-human relationship.

These are several of the challenges spiritual directors face when they meet the mysterious ways God enters into intimacy with some directees. Without the experience of these mysteries in our own spiritual lives or a vicarious openness to them through knowledge of the tradition, we really cannot be of much help to others on a passionately quickening spiritual journey.

Love Mysticism within Christian Tradition

I do not feel that spiritual directors can adequately meet the challenges outlined above without competent supervision, some knowledge of the Western Christian tradition of love mysticism, and an adequate phenomenology of desire, which relates all forms of human love to their fundamental goal of union with God. Human eros—desire—is, as Augustine recognized, unfulfilled until it rests in God. The Christian tradition of love mysticism is rooted in the biblical tradition of a personal God revealed by the self-donating love of Jesus. It draws on a personal relationship with Jesus, the Johannine Gospel and Epistles, and the Song of Songs, which Origen was the first to interpret as an allegory of the reciprocal relationship between the Word and the Christian soul. Among some of the countless mystical authors who have commented on the Song of Songs are Gregory of Nyssa, Bernard of Clairvaux, William of St. Thierry, John of the Cross, and Teresa of Avila. Augustine, in both his *Confessions* and his *Homilies on John*, made desire central to the spiritual quest. Desire remained the primary theme of Catherine of Siena's *Dialogues* as well as Julian of Norwich's *Revelations of Divine Love*.

In the medieval period, a feminine form of love mysticism, which became known as "bridal mysticism," developed. In the literature associated with bridal mysticism, women mystics describe their experiences with Jesus in highly erotic language. Written so that others might have similar experiences, the texts, such as Hadewijch's visions and poems, Gertrud the Great's *Spiritual Exercises*, and Mechthild of Magdeburg's *Flowing Light of the Godhead*, describe this path of love in great detail. Both the suffering of absence or separation from the beloved and the intensity of their unitive mystical experiences are explored.

These brief excerpts from the writings of Hadewijch, a Dutch Beguine, illustrate the fully embodied and passionate quality of this love mysticism in her Pentecost vision:

> The longing in which I then was cannot be expressed by any language or any person I know; and everything I could say about it would be unheard-of to all those who never apprehended Love as something to work for with desire, and whom Love had never acknowledged as hers. I can say this about it: I desired to have full fruition of my Beloved, and to understand and taste him to the full. I desired that his Humanity should to the fullest extent be one in fruition with my humanity, and that mine then should hold its stand and be strong enough to enter into

perfection until I content him, who is perfection itself, by purity and unity, and in all things to content him fully in every virtue. To that end I wished he might content me interiorly with his Godhead, in one spirit, and that for me he should be all that he is, without withholding anything from me. For above all the gifts that I ever longed for, I chose this gift: that I should give satisfaction in all great sufferings. For that is the most perfect satisfaction: to grow up in order to be God with God.

•   •   •   •   •

[After receiving the Eucharist] After that he came himself to me, took me entirely in his arms, and pressed me to him; and all my members felt his in full felicity, in accordance with the desire of my heart and my humanity. So I was outwardly satisfied and fully transported. [5]

While Hadewijch indicates that there is great suffering on this path of passionate love, she also describes, in the passage above, a mutual contenting with Jesus in his humanity and even sexuality (a theme chapter 5 treats). Furthermore, Hadewijch names God as Love (*minne*, feminine in gender in the Dutch), which blends and bends gender references. In the passage that follows she recommends intensifying one's longing for Love:

And if anyone then dares to fight Love with longing,
Wholly without heart and without mind,
And Love counters this longing with her longing:
That is the force by which we conquer Love. [6]

John of the Cross's mystical poetry is equally passionate:

Bride: 1   Where have you hidden,
                 Beloved, and left me moaning?
                 You fled like the stag,
                 After wounding me:
                 I went out calling you, and you were gone.

Searching for the Beloved

3 Seeking my love
I will head for the mountains and for watersides,
I will not gather flowers,
Nor fear wild beasts;
I will go beyond strong men and frontiers.

8 How do you endure
O life, not living where your live?
And being brought near death
By the arrows you receive
From that which you conceive of your beloved?

Groom: 13.3 Return, dove,
The wounded stag,
Is in sight on the hill
Cooled by the breeze of your flight.

Bride: 14 My Beloved, the mountains
And lonely wooded valleys,
Strange islands,
And resounding rivers,
The whistling of love stirring breezes,

15 The tranquil night
At the time of the rising dawn,
Silent music,
Sounding solitude,
The supper that refreshes and deepens love.

26 In the inner wine cellar
I drank of my Beloved, and when I went abroad
Through all this valley
I no longer knew anything,
And lost the herd I was following.

27   There he gave me his breast;
    There he taught me a sweet and living knowledge;
    And I gave myself to him;
    Keeping nothing back;
    And there, I promised to be his bride.

32   When you looked at me,
    Your eyes imprinted your grace in me;
    For this you loved me ardently;
    And thus my eyes deserved
    To adore what they beheld in you.

Groom: 22   The bride has entered
    The sweet garden of her desire,
    And she rests in delight,
    Laying her neck
    On the gentle arm of her Beloved.[7]

Despite the pervasiveness of this form of mysticism in both its feminine and masculine forms, Christian tradition has been ambivalent about it. The tradition has been both suspicious of sexual love and, especially in the post-Tridentine era, hostile to mystical experience, especially in this form. Celibate mystics wrote most of the mystical literature and were taught to sublimate their sexuality into disinterested love, not the ardor of passion. This often left married or single people with the impression that their embodied loving did not lead to mystical love. Furthermore, only very select groups read much of the rather large body of mystical writings related to love mysticism. For the most part, the male, celibate clergy—the primary spiritual directors of women—neither understood nor appreciated the women's tradition. In addition, few of these texts were available in good English translations until the last two decades, and the religious cultures reflected in these texts render some of them less accessible than others to the contemporary reader.

Searching for the Beloved

While intense visionary and sensory mystical experiences were extremely common and highly valued in the Middle Ages, when contemporary people (including our directees) have such experiences, they are often frightened, reluctant to discuss them, and may even confuse the mystical with the crazy. They and we continue to harbor the contradictory feelings carried in the tradition. How do we as directors spontaneously react if, for instance, one of our directees discloses a vision such as Hadewijch's or expresses sentiments such as John of the Cross's in "The Spiritual Canticle" as best representing what happened in prayer? Despite comfort or discomfort in hearing this language of passionate love mysticism, what kinds of responses facilitate their deepening intimacy with God?

Love Mysticism in the Contemporary Era

Because the Christian tradition has been ambivalent about sexual love and mystical love in the past (despite its constancy in the writings of mystics after the twelfth century), the role of desire and the relationship of human love to mystical love has become a major theme in theology and spirituality in the contemporary period, especially in the English-speaking world. Both Sebastian Moore and John Dunne have written a number of books on different facets of these questions. Systematic theologians such as Bernard Lonergan and Karl Rahner have also addressed various aspects of the unity of love of God and love of neighbor, showing that our loving ultimately leads to God.

Rahner frequently emphasizes that the fundamental experience of the believer consists not of abandonment—left to our own devices, set loose in the world, longing for a transcendent experience of love we can never have—but of invitation. The very Mystery itself solicits us, moves toward us in love and in mercy. This movement of the Mystery toward us forms the core meaning of revelation in Christian faith, as well as in Islam and Judaism. All three traditions hold that God is personal and God is love. In Christianity, that love became totally human and accessible in Jesus.

The mystical part of these three traditions encourages believers to enter fully into intimacy with this Divine Beloved. We are to become love, too. God awakens us to this divine-human love affair and initiates in us the search for the Divine Beloved. No matter how confusedly we interpret this experience, no matter how many mistakes we make along the way, no matter how often this desire for the Divine Beloved gets displaced onto other loves or other objects of desire, God continues to solicit and elicit our love. As Sebastian Moore says, "All desire [is] solicitation by the mystery we are in."[8]

The mystical process itself is the path toward illumination—toward recognizing what these desires are about, correctly interpreting them, and directing them toward the Divine. All our loves can be encompassed in this divine love, and all human loves contribute to our capacity for this divine-human intimacy. Our human loves, according to Bernard of Clairvaux, all become ordered in relation to the divine love. Whenever we fall in love, our beloved is God for us for a while. If our love is not the Divine Beloved, we will eventually be called to forgive them for not being able to be God for us. The infatuation stage of relationship typically idolizes and exalts the beloved, and although we do not intend to burden our human beloveds with these Godlike projections, the nature of desire causes us to do so. When we outgrow this stage of the relationship, these projections dissolve. Redirecting them toward God helps us emerge from illusion and release our lovers from a burden they cannot bear.[9]

It is no wonder that contemporary people often become both ambivalent and confused when their prayer experience deepens to the mystical or contemplative level on this path of love. Deprived of guidance from the earlier mystical tradition and conditioned not to expect such experiences, contemporary people are as likely to resist these experiences as to embrace them.

The Second Vatican Council finally ended the long debate about whether mystical experience was extraordinary or the normal development of a life of prayer. The council opted for the latter. Despite the increased encouragement for more mature spiritual development among the laity, many directors and directees are unfamiliar with the varieties of experience and teachings (in part, because they have been buried in a very large body of mystical texts) and with the more technical conversations going on in theological circles. The experiences, teachings, and conversations need to be expanded so that they are available to a wider audience of directors and directees.

The Mystical Process

This understanding of desire—a desire that leads us into mystical levels of prayer—in our relationship with God encompasses both theological and psychological elements. Western culture, with its emphasis on autonomy, leads us to feel isolated and longing for connection. Thus, our first step toward becoming adult lovers requires us to overcome our separateness, to develop our capacity to participate in intimate relationships, and to learn how to be with another without losing ourselves.[10] This psychological process marks the first stage in our development of affective prayer. The second step in spiritual development entails discovering an entirely new sense of "I"— one that is more my "I" than this relational ego self. This means willing and desiring with the Love that moves the universe. Unitive oneness in love requires loosening up our sense of self so that in this divine-human intimacy we no longer face our beloved as other but become one with the beloved. It leads to mutuality with God (discussed in the following chapter).

Instead of facing Jesus in imaginative contemplation, we enter into God and begin to love from within Christ, to perceive from within Christ's vision. To do so requires that we shift from contemplating Jesus as other to contemplating life from his perspective.[11] After we have overcome the emotional, physical, and psychological barriers to a shared mutuality with God, we find our true selves. At least during contemplative prayer, we find ourselves centered on God's reality instead of our own small egos. For this reason, despite all the mystical love poetry of lover and beloved, we eventually experience the Beloved directly as the source of our loving, the cause of our desirability, and the Mystery that encompasses us and all of creation. And the experience is transformative, eventually extending beyond the time of prayer to our concrete activity of care and creativity.

William, whom we met in chapter 3, exemplifies the transformative process of love mysticism. In the account that follows, he shows an awareness of the way Christ lives in him, acts in him, and is one love with him.

> Paul writes, is it cold? I have Christ with me. Is it hot? I have Christ with me. Am I sick? I have Christ with me. Am I well? You know, if someone is crying, I cry with them. If someone is happy, I will laugh with them. What Paul is really saying is if you...really are God-connected...let it snow,...let it rain, let the sun shine...whatever it is, I have that center. I have that constant connection with my beloved no matter what....
>
> I feel that I've always been called. And I say, Oh, my God. Ooh! Why me? (crying) However,...it's a love affair. If it isn't that, it is nothing, you know. Jesus is love. God is love. St. John writes that over and over again and.... Sometimes I've been so angry at the church for not being able to do a better PR job on selling love. I feel that somehow God has been short-changed because we really don't preach that this is pure loving. It's a love that is so free-

ing because real love wants growth and permits growth. Real love does not bind in chains. Real love does not possess. Evil, satanic love wants to possess you and destroy you. Divine love wants to nurture you and wants you to grow in the face of the divine person. So divine love is...to be kissed by God. (crying) Jesus is very real to me. I have kissed his feet....I've been Magdalene. I've been John with my head on his chest. I've been Peter...denying him. I've been Paul, you know...I've been that woman at the well. I've been the woman at the table saying, well, even dogs get crumbs. But Jesus is very, very real to me. It's a direct experience. I am kissing his feet. I am there with him. I come out of a meditation tradition where I'm not looking for anything. All I want to do when I meditate is to...tell God...through my mantra that...I love him. I do the catechism [phrase] "I love God with all my heart, with all my soul, with all my mind and with all my will." ...I just place myself there and...I do what Peter says: "It is a good thing to offer a spiritual sacrifice of love." Now what is a spiritual sacrifice of love? Handing over your will and saying thy will be done. You are my God. You are my creator. It is important to say, you are my Creator and I am not bothered by my crea-tureliness. I revel in it....I know that I'm created and because I'm created, I want to go to my Creator and say, "All perfect Love, you make me a creature of love. Out of love, you have redeemed me and you invite me into everlasting life." (crying) I can't ask for any more. This is it! Is there anything else? There's nothing else. So to have been created and then to be called into a divine relation-ship, I'm one with the Father, I want you to be one with me so we will all be one. Oh! One with God! Lord I'm not worthy. So when I start the day...I start the day feeling so loved.... Sometimes...I will try to praise God by doing the following...I take every atom of my body and I say it's almost as...great as the galaxy out there, right? I want every atom of my body to sing halleluias to praise God. So I feel so loved and I'm full of praise. So when I get into my car...I'm always in God's presence. I feel the presence of God when I'm driving, when I go into the classroom, you know, and what hap-pens is that, whether I like it or not, divine joy bubbles over. You can't hide it so...my students love it, you know. It's...seen by the other faculty; in other words, that guy's always happy. But I'm happy to be alive. I'm happy to love. I'm happy to be loved. I'm happy to share that love. [Jesus]...is God personified and God saying, here eat my body, drink my blood. How can you stay away from Mass? The Mass is so beautiful. The Mass is an act of love. Everything is love.[12]

The Role of Desire in Love Mysticism

According to Sebastian Moore, this transformation of the self happens through a kind of grammar of desire, a series of experiences that leads to the source of love which courses through the mystic, like a river. Moore describes this process in five steps:

1. Created by desire, I am desirable.
2. Desirable, I desire; my pleasure in myself wants to extend itself to another. Desire, in other words, does not come out of emptiness but out of fullness.
3. Since it is out of desirableness that I desire, another who causes desire in me is touching my desirableness. To cause desire is to arouse desirableness.
4. It is my desirableness, thus aroused by another, that makes me want to be desired by that other.
5. Thus the vital center of human relations is arousal; the awakening of a person's sense of being desirable, not (as commonly supposed) by being desired by another, but by being aroused by another to desire.[13]

I want to highlight three aspects of this schema. First of all, God's love really *is* the source of our desiring. We do not, however, initially feel it that way; we feel it as desire for another who may or may not requite our love. We eventually understand both cognitively and affectively, from within the mystical experience, that God's is the love that utterly and surprisingly creeps up on us from the inside. Normally, our desire is awakened from the outside, by a person who excites our longing. God's loving and desire, however, makes us desirable and causes that sense of unique worth that energizes all that we do and want to do.

Secondly, because we usually experience our desirableness indirectly, through a human beloved who loves us or whom we pursue from the abundance of our own desire, we simply remain oblivious to the first step of the process. The mystical experience, however, involves experiencing that first step directly. All that we do in spiritual practice—either through scriptural contemplation of the mysteries of faith and the reality of Jesus or through centering prayer—leads to the experience of God's desiring us. God's love moves us and moves toward us, enabling us to reciprocate that love. Hadewijch describes this process of mutual desire and response as "contenting" her beloved.[14]

The third concept I want to highlight is how spiritual desire for God differs from all other desires. Moore says:

> ...whereas desire that is simply a felt need ceases once the need is satisfied, vital desire *increases* with satisfaction. C. S. Lewis says of what he calls the sweet desire, that the one thing one longs for once the desire has gone is to have it again, to be once again aching with it. This increase of desire with fulfillment is only intelligible once we understand desire as a trustful relationship. One can always be more trustful, more connected, which means more desirous.[15]

Directors need a workable theory of the world of desire, one consonant with the mystical tradition as well as the psychological processes explored in chapter 1. Without it, directors who are uncomfortable with the love mysticism of their directees will have a very difficult time rising to this challenge.

Further study of some of the texts cited in this chapter may help both directors and their directees appropriate their experiences of love mysticism.

Ways to Address the Challenges of Love Mysticism

After discussing some central aspects of love mysticism and how they may occur in directees' divine-human intimacy with God, I offer some concrete suggestions. These correspond to the typical challenges to directors discussed in the first part of this chapter.

- Directors who have little experience with the mystical terrain of the search for the Beloved need to recognize the limits of their personal experience. A competent supervisor or consultant can reassure them that many, many historical and contemporary people have experiences related to Divine Love. They can read some of the contemporary writing about mysticism or classical mystical texts for their own background and may want to introduce some of their directees to this same literature.

- Directors themselves need to reflect on their current relationship with God. Directors who long for greater intimacy with God and find themselves blocked in this area of their own spiritual lives need to explore their feelings and desires, pursuing both the discussion and the spiritual practices around this issue with their own spiritual directors. Likewise, directors need to recognize when their anxiety about their directees' experience renders them unable to even imagine that their directees could experience even deeper intimacy with God than they currently recount in spiritual direction. The directors' avoidance of this possibility with their directees may impede their progress.

Looking away from directees when they describe experiences, changing the topic of the conversation, or simply listening without making any response that might facilitate the directees' deeper intimacy with God are typical anxious responses. Directors may even discourage the directees by advising them "not to let this happen again."

A more helpful response on the part of the director might include asking questions to explore the depth of the encounter further. These might elicit their directees' sense of intensity, their comfort or discomfort with getting even closer to God, their feelings in response to unitive experience, and their perception about how the encounter concluded. For example, when a directee reports an intense exchange of love between herself and Jesus conveyed by a look in a visual contemplation, the director could explore what the directee considers *intense* to be. The director could explore whether the looking ever gives way to touching. In the same situation, a director could inquire about how close or how far away the two are from each other or ask if it would it be comfortable for the directee to move closer to Jesus. In an experience in which, instead of images, some sensory description such as "I felt an inflow of love in my being" provides the medium of encounter with God, a director could ask for more elaboration, especially about what it felt like to receive this love.

For both types of experiences, directors could helpfully explore how the experience came to an end. Frequently, they will discover that the directee moved away from the experience before the mystical interlude came to a natural end—a common and subtle form of resistance. Directors need to understand that there is always a further place to go in divine-human intimacy, even if it is only staying with an experience of God five minutes longer before moving away from it.

- Spiritual directors who feel jealous or envious of their directees need to acknowledge and explore these feelings in their own spiritual direction or supervision. Feelings of envy suggest that the director needs to address his or her own frustrated desire for intimacy with God by bringing this awareness to prayer. Often a directee who evokes these feelings is grace for the director. Envy serves as a potential spiritual invitation to the director. Such a director also needs to become curious enough to explore the directee's experience in greater detail. In order to do so, he or she will need to be more consciously present to God.

- When directees are neither praying nor reporting religious experiences while at the same time expressing the desire to pray or for greater intimacy with God, their frustrated directors need to stay with whatever desires are present within them. A careful exploration of any desire will, if properly understood, lead to the directee's deeper desire and possibly reveal what is blocking its realization. According to John of the Cross, the lack of events in prayer coupled with desire for God and concern about the situation is one of several signs indicating the beginning of infused contemplation. Directees are likely either to reveal some form of sinfulness causing them to avoid prayer or a more confusing—yet subtle, deep, and clear—desire for God, similar to the woman in chapter 1 who discovered her sense of blessing and gratitude when she went beyond her conditioned desires.

- An understanding of the subtlety and confusion about desires in the directee can help a director who too easily assumes that the directee knows what grace to pray for. The director might examine the entire conversation for clues to the directee's desires, which may not be entirely conscious. It is important for directors to ask their directees: "What does God desire for you?" as well as "What do you desire?" The question about God's desires for the directee may reveal whether or not the directee is approaching a unitive experience with God that results in mutuality (explored in the next chapter). Such unitive experiences lead to a God-human partnership with feelings of equality, reciprocity, giving to God as well as receiving, and mutual care and pleasuring. Directors need to explore not only what the directee wants, but also whether or not the directee is willing to embrace the changes or implications that would result from receiving what is desired.

- Both directors and directees may collude in assuming that love mysticism is a relic from the past and not something that happens to contemporary people. A male directee like William confounds gender expectations as well. Both director and directee can become surprised and frightened by the manifestations of passionate love in divine-human intimacy. Directors need to educate themselves in the tradition and deal with their own resistances to these experiences. By doing so, they can facilitate for their directees the process of deepening intimacy with God in whatever form the experience takes. Sometimes resistance to the language of passionate love manifests itself; sometimes directors simply fear the unfamiliar or have difficulty with passion and intimacy of any kind. The same resistances may be present in the directee. Often they will need a great deal of reassurance to surrender to these experiences and not evade them.

• When directees have unitive experiences, directors need to probe them. God often seems paradoxically present and absent, simultaneously as well as alternatively. This seeming absence is a frequent experience in love mysticism. Diane's description illustrates this feature of love mysticism perfectly:

> I'd have to say for about the past year and a half I've been most aware of...God's absence. It has been emptiness, longing, darkness, and there have been times when we did come together, and it was like color in a black and white scene for me. What I notice the most is that I feel empty. And when we're together, it will be something small in the environment that suddenly becomes *loaded*. Music is always very important. The images come [from] the texts [of songs]....The image and the Scripture accompanied by the emotion and the music will suddenly be riveting. And I could stay with one image for over six months. [One was] God as the hiding place. The text was, "He will hide me in the shelter of his tents all the days of my life." That image from the psalms of being camped about and besieged—I listened to relentlessly. What happened inside was quite hard to put in words. It was not an experience of God as the strength and the safety and the stronghold and shield. It was more of a reaching out to that. It was not the affirmation of it. It was, please let this be so. I hope like anything this is so. It was a reaching out. Some comfort for me. Some lessening of tension inside. But a really deeply

tearful longing. That's what I felt. Emptiness. And there's something about the image of the tent...[which] is that same [way] its a form but it's empty. My soul didn't have a place to be, and I wanted a place to be with God. There was an ache but it was more...from the human experience of the reaching off into the nothing. I hope like hell there's something there. When the shift comes, I experience... God moving toward [me]. Then the prayer is a relaxation and a receiving and an affirming. It would come in an image to me. It's as if I've been standing out on the cliff of my soul. Like this, hands out, reaching. All my hope is to touch something...[which] may or may not come. Then something is coming toward me and answering. I'd say that the music I listened to for a long time [was like that]. There is something about the smallness of the details that has been speaking to me. Simplicity, smallness, insignificance, dearness. It's not like seeing a homeless person on the street and crying. It's even more elemental than that. Like ducks in the pond. It's not the issue of homelessness or human suffering; it's just something that is its own self. And that something takes you to the heart of reality. I'm very aware that it comes through tiny [manifestations]. I would interpret that according to one of the Sufis who says, "...when you want God that badly you will find God in the least envelope of time." The contact that is so charged is usually extremely brief. A second, two seconds, ten seconds. What happens from that contact can roll for a day, two days, a week. It's a very tight bud of experience. And it unpetals, unpetals. It's bigger on the inside than it is on the outside.[16]

Is this an experience of absence or is it more accurately a new way of being in God or Jesus? Is the directee no longer "seeing" Jesus because Jesus is indwelling and transforming the person? Directors may help directees more easily notice ways that God is acting in and through them by using the language of "sensing" rather than "seeing." Finally, the director can encourage the directee to stay present to God, using a very simple prayer form.

The two mystical paths—one full of events, images, desire, and the other less eventful, usually without images or intense feelings discussed above—require quite different responses. The first path, which resembles romantic love and is often characterized by an alternation of presence and absence, is usually filled with events. Directees need to be encouraged to take all of them and none of them seriously and guided to ever deepening surrender and mutuality. Eventually this path leads to an experience of self deeper than the superficial ego, to the self that is already the beloved of God.[17] The authenticity of these experiences lies not in the experiences, but in the transformation of the life as a whole. The director listens with an ear for the signs of liberating grace (listed in chapter 3). The directees' descriptions of their lives, behaviors, and dispositions embedded in their narratives will disclose the fruits of the divine-human intimacy. Typically, these will be the gifts and fruits of the Holy Spirit.

It is also important for the director neither to discount nor trivialize the painful yearning of passion. Recent commentary on the teaching of the thirteenth-century Beguine, Hadewijch, discloses that the voicing of passionate desire conquers love.[18] Part of the director's role is to encourage the voicing of the longing and a direct approach to intimacy. God *does* make love with quite human beloveds in unmistakable ways. The director's role does not include deciding how God can or cannot allure and love the directee but, rather, staying with the directee's experience.

The second apophatic path of a paradoxical absence/presence requires the director to encourage the directee's fidelity to intentionality toward God by regular contemplative prayer despite a lack of "events." A director can support the directee by gentle probing of the prayer experience for subtle changes in affectivity, awareness, or consciousness and by exploring life events in a holistic manner to notice the "fruits" of the directee's contemplative prayer in action and affectivity. The director should also explore all negative emotions in the directee—frustration, impatience, unrequited desire, envy, or boredom—so that these emotions remain conscious lest they lead the directee to distance him- or herself from God. Avoidance of these feeling states may result in a directee's abandoning prayer just when persistence in prayer is most important.

- Director anxiety about the directee's erotic and romantic attachments can deprive the directee of self-understanding and response to divine-human intimacy. Often, addictive, disordered, or "love crazy" situations are divine-human intimacy wanting to happen. The director needs to remain conscious and reflective about feelings and judgments related to the directee's relationships. Reflection and exploration of these reactions in supervision frequently enable the director to become less anxious and freer to help the directee connect the desires expressed in interpersonal relationships to desire for intimacy with God.

Explicit conversation about erotic experiences and desires related to divine-human intimacy or to other relationships may also evoke anxiety in a director who interprets this topic as an indication that a directee has fallen in love with him or her. In this case, careful supervision can support the director in testing this assumption, in maintaining appropriate boundaries, and in avoiding sexual involvement with a directee. All loves can lead to God and be harmonized in divine-human intimacy, but this process happens over time and often requires therapy to sort it through.

- Prior history shapes expectations about relationships and intimacy as well as patterns of behavior in intimate relationships. Directees bring expectations and patterns of behavior into their relationship with God and may need to change some of them. Just as directors need to explore their directees' relational and sexual histories in relationship to any blocks preventing progressive intimacy with God, so too, directors need to explore aspects of their own relational history if they are avoiding these areas with their directees.

Directors can be extremely helpful to their directees who are experiencing love mysticism in their religious experience. It is equally important for directors to pay attention to the spiritual as well as psychological challenges they encounter when they work with directees who are flourishing in divine-human intimacy. John Dunne, a well-known contemporary theologian who has explored desire in a series of books, offers an autobiographical description of the process of unknowing desiring, which reveals the desire within all our desires. He reminds all of us that there is much that remains mysterious and unknowing about this divine-human intimacy.

There is a desire in all our desires, I believe, an enthusiasm in all our enthusiasms. It is an unknowing love of God. It is what I may call "my ancient soul of a child." To hear that love in all our loves is to hear "ancient voices of children," and I may have to go very far along love's road to know it and to love with a love that is knowing....

As love becomes more knowing, or more knowingly "unknowing," as I learn to discern the love of God in all our loves, I become more peaceful about love not being consummated in possession, about the words I love not being mine, about the music I love not being mine, about the friend I love not being mine alone. It is consummated rather in being "one with God" who belongs to all, who is "mine own, and not mine own."[19]

FOR FURTHER REFLECTION:

- What is your relational history with intimacy and erotic experience?
- Do any of your assumptions about God or the spiritual life inhibit your ability to companion directees who are anxious about or enjoying erotic experience in their divine-human intimacy?
- Has envy of your directees' religious experience ever emerged in your direction sessions? If so, how have you felt about your reaction in light of your directee's experience and your own spiritual longings?
- What is your level of comfort in hearing about the full range of sexually explicit relationships your directees may need to talk about?
- Can you recognize the path of love in both its expressive form and its less eventful form?
- Are you equally comfortable accompanying directees on either of the two mystical paths without privileging one over the other?

NOTES

1. Kenneth Cragg, *The Wisdom of the Sufis* (New York: New Directions, 1976), LX, 48.

2. Ibid., CXXXVIII, 86.

3. See Walter E. Conn, *The Desiring Self: Rooting Pastoral Counseling and Spiritual Direction in Self-Transcendence* (Mahwah, N.J.: Paulist Press, 1998), for perceptive descriptions of these various understandings of the self from a psychological perspective and their relationship to the human existential drive toward self-transcendence in knowledge, love, and action.

4. Some readers may find Bernard McGinn's treatment of this type of mysticism helpful. See *The Flowering of Mysticism: Men and Women in the New Mysticism*—1200–1550, vol. 3 of *The Presence of God: A History of Western Christian Mysticism* (New York: Crossroad, 1998), especially chapters 4 and 5. See also Carol Lee Flinders, *Enduring Grace: Living Portraits of Seven Women Mystics* (San Francisco: Harper, 1993) for a more popular treatment.

5. *Hadewijch: The Complete Works*, trans. Mother Columba Hart, Classics of Western Spirituality (Mahwah, N.J.: Paulist Press, 1980), vision 7, 280–82.

6. Ibid., "Poems in Stanzas," poem 38, ll. 53–56.

7. "The Spiritual Canticle" in *John of the Cross: Selected Writings*, Classics of Western Spirituality, trans. Kieran Kavanaugh (Mahwah, N.J.: Paulist Press, 1987) 221–27, stanzas indicated in text.

8. Sebastian Moore, *Jesus, Liberator of Desire* (New York: Crossroad, 1989), 11.

9. Etty Hillesum's journal, *An Interrupted Life*, provides an explicit example of this process in her spiritual development.

10. See pp. 53 through 74 of David Schnarch, *Passionate Marriage: Keeping Love and Intimacy Alive in Committed Relationships* (New York: Owl Books, 1997) for a psychological description of differentiation in intimate relationships that avoids both fusion with the other or exaggerated separateness.

11. See Beatrice Bruteau, *Radical Optimism* (New York: Crossroad, 1993) and *The Easter Mysteries* (New York: Crossroad,

1995), for descriptions and meditative processes that foster this development.

12. Used with permission.

13. Sebastian Moore, *Let This Mind Be in You* (Minneapolis: Winston Press, 1985), 44.

14. *Hadewijch*, letter 16, nos. 9, 14.

15. Moore, *Jesus, Liberator of Desire*, 11. This synopsis of Moore's thought cannot do justice to it; directors who want to understand his analysis more thoroughly will want to read both this volume and *Let This Mind Be in You* (see n. 13).

16. Used with permission from a thirty-eight-year-old single mother.

17. This theme became very important in Henri Nouwen's later writings; see especially *Life of the Beloved: Spiritual Living in a Secular World* (New York: Crossroad, 1996).

18. John Giles Milhaven, *Hadewijch and Her Sisters* (Albany: State University of New York Press, 1993).

19. John S. Dunne, *Love's Mind* (Notre Dame, Ind.: University of Notre Dame Press, 1993), 83.

Chapter 5

MUTUALITY WITH GOD: "WHERE BELOVED AND LOVED ONE SHALL WHOLLY FLOW THROUGH EACH OTHER"

The words above,[1] from the thirteenth-century mystic Hadewijch, beautifully evoke the goal of the spiritual journey short of resurrection. This mutuality is an important aspect of what Hadewijch described in one of her visions as "growing up to be God with God." As the mystical process progresses beyond the beginnings to a predominately unitive relationship with God, a sense of profound mutuality with God begins to become prominent. "Becoming God with God," as Hadewijch alternatively called this experience, is usually rather startling to directees and their directors. They may find it so because their appropriation of theology and the mystical tradition, in many cases, remains uninformed by the mystical experience and teaching of mature mystics. As a result, many directors miss this developing mutuality in some of their directees because they have been conditioned not to expect it. The occurrence of mystical experience that disconfirms the expectations of both director and directee may, at first, evoke dismissal of or resistance to God's increasing initiations toward a more mutual relationship with such directees.

Intimacy with God, like intimacy with significant others in our lives, is characterized by being and expressing one's self while in the presence of one who is important to us. When intimate self-disclosure is mutual, both partners reveal themselves and receive the other without fusion or flight. A greater stability of loving connection thus becomes possible. For such intimacy to develop, however, feelings of inequality, either related to power or desire for one another, must eventually be overcome. Because God is by nature transcendent, we first experience God as dramatically, numinously, and powerfully Other. Few of us quite grasp that the process of mystical transformation gradually overcomes this sense of the utter Otherness of God in favor of a radical mutuality with God.

If directors neither recognize nor understand that a developing mutuality with God actually signals the beginning of mystical development (what the Spanish mystics called transforming union), they may actually hinder the relational change God is beginning to effect. Rather than occasional and transient unitive experiences with God, the oneness with God described by directees such as William (in the preceding chapter) begins to become stable and consistent, at first during times of prayer or retreat and subsequently as an ongoing experience. Most directees who recognize this shift respond in disbelief and often fear. While only God can effect this change in directees, directors can allay their directees' anxiety and support them in responding to God's initiative, but only if they themselves understand this development and encourage directees to cooperate with God's action and respond in increasingly mutual ways.

Despite the solid witness to it in the mystical tradition, mutuality has been a neglected theme. Considerably more explanation is required to clarify why we have failed to see it and why we are now beginning to recognize it more clearly. In feminist theological reflection, mutuality has ignited the desire, of women particularly, to understand how relationships within the Christian community ought to be structured. Before being restructured on the basis of Mediterranean patriarchy, the pattern of relationship among members of the early community gathered around Jesus was clearly a "discipleship of equals."[2] As feminist scholars appropriated this basic scriptural insight they discovered in mystical texts, especially those written by women, that God also desires a relationship of radical mutuality with human beings.

This theme of mutuality with God has been well hidden. We have little familiarity with it and have not heard much about it. Yet, this insight and the self-God images that express it need to be more clearly understood and affect our practice of spiritual direction.

Preliminary Considerations

I want to consider briefly three preliminary topics related to the theme of mutuality with God.

Correlation Between Self-Image and God-Image

First, there is always a correlation between our self-image and our image of God. As we undergo the process of growth and development, our sense of ourselves forms and reforms on the basis of our experience. Automatically, our self-image sets up a correlative image-pair with who God is to us, whether explicit or not. Spiritual directors have long been aware of how our self-image and our God-image correspond. God relates to us in and through this pair of correlative images. God is not, of course, restricted to any image; no image exhausts the reality of God. But we *do* image.

Development, change, or growth in one's self-image is a psychological prerequisite not only for a positively construed relationship with God, but also for the radical mutuality with God that Jesus mediates for us. This mutuality comes to fruition during the more mature stages of mystical development. Spiritual directors can support this deepening intimacy with God by fostering the emergence of images of mutuality, such as the scriptural image of Jesus or God as friend. Damage to self-image through abuse, victimization, or impaired psychological development can prove difficult to overcome when attempting to relate to God beyond the negative God-image that correlates with the negative self-image.

Mutuality with God in this context is not what philosophers mean by an ontological equality with God. We never share the same *being*; we are never equal or mutual in this sense. Rather, I am describing what the relationship with God feels like when it becomes more mutual. The more we grow in the spiritual life, the more the feeling of inequality is overcome by God's gracing us. God increases our capacity for God so that relational mutuality becomes possible. Thus, the sense of God's transcendence may recede in our experience and be replaced by an incredible mutuality and partnership. Dorothy's case, which follows, illustrates this shift, while William's narrative (in chapter 4) includes images of mutuality and a strong sense of God's transcendence. Most of us have been taught not to believe in this graced capability.

Most of us have been taught that we can never overcome this gap between God and ourselves. St. Paul tells us that we become "a new creation in Christ." New creation might suggest how God overcomes this gap by making a new relationship possible by grace. I image this as Jesus relinquishing equality with God so that we can become more Godlike. We are to grow into a graced reality, which is more than we start out to be but which exists potentially from the beginning. I think this is true for all of us, no matter how whole or damaged our personal backgrounds might be.

Effect of Language about God

Second, language about God can either limit our sense of Divine Reality or imaginatively expand it. Our image of God can either make it harder or easier for God to reveal God's self in radically loving ways. The way we, as spiritual directors, talk about or image God can either create a straightjacket for God or open new and endless possibilities and imaginative freedom in us and our directees for God to be God-for-us—utterly surprising, new and fresh, no longer held within our narrow confines. An exclusive use of images of inequality or nonreciprocity maintains a power over our imaging process that makes it more difficult to recognize a graced movement toward mutuality with God.

Negative or inaccurate images for God maintain unjust social relations on the human plane as well as emotional distance between God and humans. What is the correlative image, for example, if we speak of Jesus or God as Lord? Servant, slave, or subject? We don't relate well to that in our culture. We don't want to admit that there are authorities or that we owe them something. This image goes against the grain of our democratic instincts. What about Jesus as leader where the paired image is disciple or follower? But what about ourselves as leaders? If God is a monarch, we are once again subjects. What if we image Jesus as friend or lover? Then we become his friends or lovers. Although these images are not without their own limitations, they promote affective immediacy and mutuality rather than distance and inequality. As spiritual directors we are responsible for how we talk about God and whether we contribute to the deformation of God's image or the continual evocation of more adequate images of God's reality.

Gender Differences

Third, because of our concrete social histories women and men develop different self-/God-images based on gender construction.[3] Roman Catholicism continues to assign exclusively male gender to God in public speech and in liturgical worship. If you happen to be a woman, this linguistic usage sets up interesting possibilities and difficulties in experiencing oneself as truly in the image of God. Women are not invited to appropriate a Godlike self. In fact, women are even wrongly told that because of our female embodiment, we cannot image Christ, denying our actual experience of Christic life initiated in baptism. Men, on the other hand, tend to assume unconsciously that they are already Godlike. Men are in the image of God as the birthright of their male embodiment.[4]

The spiritual tradition has handled this in different ways depending upon whether it is addressing men or women. As part of the conversion process, men must empty themselves, like Jesus did, of their social "Godlikeness" in order to be in right relationship to a transcendent God. One reason some men are never attracted to religion lies in their recognition that they have to relinquish some form of masculine power. Because of their greater social power, men often forget that they are not themselves God but only in the image of God. Mutuality with God becomes possible only after a man clearly relinquishes the idolatry culturally constructed for him.

Some men, especially those in the late adolescent and young adulthood stages of masculine development, may feel as if the conversion process requires them to become "unmanly." Men who embrace the spiritual quest seem to place their masculinity in jeopardy.[5] In the *Exercises*, Ignatius seems to be acutely aware of this threat and uses images from male experience with great subtlety and ingenuity. Using images from military and courtly life, Ignatius subverts stereotypical masculine attitudes and instead fosters a deconstruction and restructuring of masculine identity in relationship to the creator God and to Christ.

In their conversion process, on the other hand, women first develop sufficient self-esteem to experience themselves as enjoying full personhood. Typically, this includes a sense of agency and dignity. Women already stand in appropriate relationship to transcendence because of their social conditioning. Women do not immediately assume they are like God; they already know what it is to be earthly and not quite Godlike. The spiritual task for women is to become fully themselves.

If a woman makes the Exercises with a director who has little sensitivity to gender differences, she is initially exercised in the consideration of a "manly" form of discipleship. A woman's psyche does interesting and creative things with this dilemma. It is important not to underestimate the ability of a directee's imaginative psyche to create the images needed in the process of transformation. People will create the images they need and find ways of making the Exercises through those images. One of the most helpful things directors can do is to respect and foster this internal creativity. In the imaginative contemplations of the Exercises, many women directors and men, too, re-present and re-describe the process as appropriately as possible through the images emerging in their directees.

Nevertheless, it is only with great difficulty that some women may discover the images of self and God needed to claim themselves as being in the image of God. The woman in chapter 1 who made her whole retreat contemplating how Jesus loves with a mother's love was doing just this. She recognized a profound connection between Jesus' agapic love and her own maternal love. Both she and Jesus were maternal in significant ways.

Careful attention to gendered images of God is just as important in ongoing spiritual direction. A much greater variety of images suitable for women are available today, and happily, they are also more widely known. Most women do not need metaphors of self-emptying and abasement, but rather images that strengthen their sense of self and agency. Masculine images may be of little help to a woman who cannot or maybe even should not identify with them. Spiritual directors either support this imaginative creativity and freedom in their female directees or discourage it by their responses.

Masculine images of God also pose complex challenges to both men and women depending on their sexual orientations. Gay men and heterosexual women find it easier to integrate their erotic desires for unitive love in their prayer to and contemplation of Jesus. Gay men, however, may have difficulty believing in God's good-willing and benevolence toward them if their fathers have been harsh or rejecting. The father-son relationship for both gay and heterosexual men is often one of neither intimacy nor unconditional love.

Exclusively masculine images of God evoke different responses in our psyches depending on our gendered starting point. A woman who has been abused by her father or other adult men will also have difficulty with a Father-God image or any other masculine image. Susan, whose verbatim ended chapter 1, struggled with a troubled relationship to her father. Her most healing and intimate images were exquisite feminine personifications of God that emerged spontaneously in her prayer. For many years, she also enjoyed consistent images of Jesus.

Mutuality with God

Lesbian women and heterosexual men may be unable to integrate erotic desire in their prayer without the availability of a feminine image of God. This explains why Mary often plays such a large role in some men's spiritual experience, Ignatius's included. It is, however, sometimes difficult to think about Mary in a sexual way. She is available for many only in a very limited way for such projections, particularly if she is too exclusively identified with the maternal. Ignatius, for example, projected all of his mothering needs onto Mary, for his own mother had died when he was young. While he had considerable attraction to women in a variety of ways throughout his life, he sublimated much of this desire for the feminine toward Mary and encouraged retreatants to include Mary and the saints in their colloquies and contemplations. Some male directees, though, do relate to images of Mary in a desirous way. Those who do discover their sexualized imaging of Mary may be embarrassed to disclose it in the spiritual direction conversation unless the director invites such a possibility.

A new feminine God-image for both Jesus and God now emerging is *Sophia*. Using this image, some men and women are able to develop an intimate loving relationship in contemplation. It is very important for a spiritual director to identify particular Jesus- or God-images that can comfortably carry a retreatant's erotic energies. These energies are the human, instinctual root of our insatiable desire for the Other, who is ultimately God. If this channel is blocked in prayer, those whose erotic longing is not fulfilled by a particular human beloved may never really develop a sufficiently great love— one capable of being filled with God. If we do not integrate these erotic longings in our prayer, we may diminish our capacity for entering into this intimacy with God.

The Pre-Reformation Mystical Tradition as a Resource for Images of God

Pre-Reformation strands of the spiritual tradition are full of images that strengthen women's sense of self. Joan of Arc's voices infused her with courage and tenacity. Gertrud's visions confirmed her gifts of spiritual direction and counsel. Catherine of Siena discovered God as Truth and Jesus as the Bridge leading to salvation. Jesus healed, consoled, strengthened, comforted, and commissioned these women. Texts written by visionary women reveal a fluidity of God-images that are masculine, feminine, or organic (from nature). These not only encouraged, but also required, the women to dare partnering with the Divine. The God-images arising from their religious experience offered them continual reassurance when summoned to act for and with God in ways their culture discouraged. These images, especially those of Christ and Mary, healed damaged or weak self-images and fostered increasingly mutual interactions. The exchange of hearts between Jesus and many of these mystical women imaged this mutuality. The mystic, thereafter, loved with the heart of Jesus. He gives himself to her and she to him. They join together in a redemptive partnership for the world.

The gender identifications for God was much more fluid in the imagery from the medieval period than the imagery from the Reformation or Modern periods. In medieval imagery, love was often personified as feminine, as we have seen for both Hadewijch and Mechthild. Christ had both masculine and feminine qualities, Mary was often a covert feminine God-image,[6] and the Holy Spirit took every imaginable form. Men, too, in the pre-Reformation period benefited from a greater variety in gender identifications. Thus, a Francis of Assisi could marry Lady Poverty and relate to creation through both masculine and feminine personifications.

In summary, these three preliminary considerations sharpen our awareness as spiritual directors of the complexity and creativity of internally and externally generated imagery in facilitating mutuality with God. Our self-image and God-image are correlative to one another. Language about God can either limit or expand how we imagine God. Gender and sexual orientation, too, profoundly conditions our sense of self and image of God. As directors, we can carefully work with this delicate representation of our directees' relationship with God.

Rediscovery of the Theme of Mutuality with God

What might help us, as spiritual directors, to better appropriate the neglected theme of mutuality with God? Recovering some images from this earlier tradition helps us recognize that this is neither an aberration nor a contemporary fad. Recognizing this theme in later historical periods supports a positive response to its emergence. Using language about God that portrays this kind of relationship as not only possible, but as the actual goal of both the salvation offered in Jesus and the goal of the mystical path helps directors and directees become open to such an experience. Noticing this theme in our own experience and that of our directees makes us more comfortable with it.

My discovery of this theme occurred first in my own prayer, which was increasingly difficult to interpret due to the unexpectedness and originality of its imagery. Instead of looking at Jesus in interior vision, Jesus disappeared from view, but I could sense or feel him illumining me and loving me from within. In my teaching or spiritual direction, I would have an even clearer sense of when Jesus was guiding me or acting through me. At first I didn't even notice the shift in imagery because I did not think God could be like this. Not having imagined God could want a mutual relationship with me, I was disoriented. I had failed to notice it in the classical texts that had most influenced me. As this sense of intimacy and mutuality developed further, some of my images changed again. In one, I was riding *Sophia*-Christ's chariot, first across the seas and then lifted by the winds. In the image, Christ was embracing me from behind in the chariot, holding the reigns with me. The holding alternated between riding together and mutual embrace, but the chariot moved all the while. This image and others that followed, which included a sense of walking side by side in my daily round, give something of the feeling of intimacy, connection, partnership, and shared activity.

While the theme and imagery of mutuality clearly appeared in the classical texts, I had been taught to pay more attention to other images and teachings. Two writers greatly influenced a shift in my awareness. John Giles Milhaven's book *Hadewijch and Her Sisters: Other Ways of Loving and Knowing* provided a helpful philosophical analysis of the mutuality of love and the bodily knowing from which it emerges. An article by Constance FitzGerald in which she traced this same theme in Teresa of Avila and John of the Cross was also significant.[7]

Ignatian Tradition

When I taught a class on Ignatius subsequent to this shift in awareness, I looked for Ignatius's version of mutuality. I found it most clearly expressed in points 1 and 2 of the "Contemplation to Attain Love,"[8] but also in the contemplations that culminate the retreat:

> The first is that love ought to manifest in deeds rather than in words.[9]

Mutuality with God

The second is that love consists in a mutual sharing of goods, for example, the lover gives and shares with the beloved what he possesses, or something of that which he has or is able to give; and vice versa, the beloved shares with the lover. Hence, if one has knowledge, he shares it with the one who does not possess it; and so also if one has honors, or riches. Thus, one always gives to the other.[10]

Love in these contemplations is very concrete. Love does not constitute a feeling, but rather a mutuality of actions and a sharing of goods. Climaxing the highly unitive third and fourth weeks, these contemplations highlight Christ's sharing all with the retreatant. Depending on the retreatant's stage of spiritual development, he or she may experience an enlargement of capacity to join with Christ in this mutuality as a fruit of the contemplations.

Often missed, though, is the trinitarian context of all of these contemplations. Initially, they are extremely Christo-centric—Jesus is God drawing near to us in mutuality. But the goal of this final contemplation is to expand that mutuality from ourselves and Christ to ourselves with God as well, available for the Spirit to work in and through us. If we are able to respond, we are brought together with Jesus into a relationship of mutuality with God. For some retreatants, this "Contemplation to Attain Love," which is the end and goal of the retreat, might be used as the "First Principle and Foundation"—an alternative description of right relationship with God and creation.

Ignatius's own vision at La Storta, which occurred shortly before he arrived in Rome to seek papal approval of the Society of Jesus and which confirmed his mission, embodied this mutuality. In the vision, Ignatius contemplates Mary, asking her to "place him with her son" in the heavenly court. The imagery of a courtier captures Ignatius's union with God in terms of his masculine identity. Placed by a "Queenly Mary" (most likely an implicit feminine God-image), Ignatius is accepted into the royal court as a companion of Jesus—a sibling adopted by the King and Queen—to live the rest of his days in familial intimacy with the Trinity and friendship with Jesus.

Ignatius's company would participate in the same deeds of redemptive love as Christ's body on earth. To our twenty-first-century ears this imagery may not sound as intimate or as mutual as it felt to Ignatius. We tend to feel the distance royal imagery creates, but what is happening to Ignatius is acceptance into the royal family. In these images of sharing Christ's affections, ministry, redemptive love, and resurrected hope, we discover the best culturally available masculine images of the male-male mutual relationship for Ignatius. Thereafter, clearly guided by his ongoing, continuous experience of God's presence, Ignatius not only finds God in all things but also finds all things already in God.

Ignatius's images for this goal of the *Exercises* enabled him to truly experience God in all things—the entire created universe whose stars he loved to contemplate, the interpersonal world of the Company of Jesus, and the Spirit-vivified community in and through which he was to partner Christ in the service of others. Ignatius utters his "Suscipe" ["Take, Lord, Receive..."][11] precisely in this context of experienced mutuality with God, "the mutual sharing of goods." This is his response (and the retreatants') to this mutual relationship. I think we and our retreatants too often try to say these words before we experience this mutuality and such sentiments arise spontaneously.

Additional Examples from the Late Medieval Tradition

Ignatius's images of mutuality provide an excellent example of mutuality within masculine consciousness. A number of women mystics from the late medieval period exemplify feminine versions of mutuality. For instance, Hadewijch of Brabant, the thirteenth-century Beguine, offered this poem, which promised the eventual fulfillment of love's goal, to her audience during a time of great suffering.

> O hearts, let not your many griefs
> Distress you! You shall soon blossom;
> You shall row through all storms,
> Until you come to that luxuriant land
> Where Beloved and loved one shall wholly flow through each other:
> Of that, noble fidelity is your pledge here on earth.[12]

Mechthild of Magdeburg is no less daring in her descriptions of mutuality with God:

> God has so enfolded the soul into him/herself and so poured out the divine nature completely into it that the soul is rendered speechless. It says nothing except that God is in the closest communion with it and God is more than a Father. [13]

> God lays the soul in his glowing heart so that He, the great God, and she, the humble maid, embrace and are united as thoroughly as water is with wine.[14]

> As love grows and expands in the soul, it rises eagerly to God and overflows toward the Glory which bends towards it. Then Love melts through the soul into the senses, so that the body too might share in it, for Love is drawn into all things.[15]

Notice how Mechthild conceives of the embrace of God in the Trinity through these images of mutuality. God is more than a Father. She, the humble maid, overflows toward the Glory that bends toward her. The attraction is clearly mutual; God bends toward her and she flows back toward the Glory.

This is not a purely "spiritual" experience but one that her body shares.

The emphasis in many women mystics on the enjoyment of the Beloved often conceals the fact that, like most of us, they lived active apostolic lives. As Milhaven emphasizes, these women came to know the Divine Beloved in continuity with and through the analogies most characteristic of family life—feeding and nurturing, nursing someone through an illness, the way one knows a person through the contours of their body and the approach of their footsteps.

Mutuality in loving makes lovers vulnerable to one another. This way of knowing results in joy and pleasure in the presence of one's beloved. Absence of the beloved evokes feelings of grief and sometimes anxiety. Mutual joy can become mutual sorrow and vice versa. When one's child flourishes, so too is the parent pleasured. When the child is sick or injured, the parent suffers with the child. The distance between God and humanity is overcome through Jesus' incarnation, death, resurrection, and the gift of indwelling Spirit. Mystically, one comes to experience this gift of intimacy with God through mutuality with Jesus first, usually, and then with the Godhead, whom Jesus manifests.

Dorothy's Imagery

Some contemporary examples of these kinds of movements in the retreat context might make this more concrete. Dorothy gives the following account of a retreat she made in her late forties. Her imagery reflects this movement toward mutuality with Jesus and with the persons of the Trinity, clearly illustrating the reformation of her self-image in the process of her spiritual growth. The images are lively, humorous, earthy, and grounded in her originality. So powerful and effective were the graces of these breakthrough experiences, that, four years after the events, she was moved to tears as she described them in our interview.

It was as though I was in a jungle. There was this swamp. The mud was human excrement; it wasn't just mud. It was my stuff. So here I was and I was frightened and I couldn't move. My heart was pounding, everything was happening. And I tried to lean against a tree, and the tree moved because there was a snake around it. There was nowhere I could go and I was stuck in there. Then out of the mud there was a dragon that was coming after me. It was getting closer and closer. [In] the meantime, Jesus has been away for years, like two or three years. [She had been angry at God for some time for having disappeared prior to this experience.] Jesus arrives just in the nick of time. There's a really big struggle with the dragon and they're twisting in the mud and they're getting all messy. And Jesus is able to take the dragon's mouth and he snaps it and he's twisting the dragon's neck. But both of them go under and they didn't come back. They're gone. Now I'm crying and I can't move, I am so petrified. Then the jungle begins to dry up and wither. The only thing left was the desert. I was standing there, and I wouldn't leave. I was crying. At that moment the desert became a very holy place for me because I could see...the combat of death in the Easter sequence there. That had happened and I couldn't go away from there. Well, along came Jesus. And I was looking over here and he comes the other way. I looked at him and I didn't know what to say. He was caked in mud. And I'll just never forget, he had a streak that came from out of his ear, across his face like that. It was just awful. And the prayer session ended at that point. I had tried to say stuff from the gospel like Thomas, "my Lord and my God" and kneel down and all that. So I went to [my director] with this and I said what happened. And he listened. I don't know if you know him well enough to know how his face is so open. He listens to you but he's not making any judgments at all. So with his very open face and his gentle voice he sent me back to pray and he said, "Ask Jesus how you can minister to him." So I did go back and said that. And he said, "You know, I want to have a bath." So I said, "All right." I go over and get the towels and soap, I bring it over, I'm ministering to Jesus. Then he takes them and all that, and he says, "You know, you need a bath too." He picks me up. There was an oasis there and into the water we went. And I washed him, He washed me. It was really all right. (crying)

How transparent these images of mutuality are! "My Lord, and my God" were not words that expressed it at all. Rather, her images show reciprocity and an overcoming of distance and a difference in status in her relationship with Jesus.

The following narrative, from a different retreat, was part of the same movement Dorothy described as "becoming friends with God." It shows how the process of the retreat healed her damaged self-image. Prior to the retreat, some good therapy helped her understand how issues related to her family of origin were affecting her. The retreat seems to reflect her integration of a new self-understanding with her religious experience. The change in both her self-image and her relationship to it are quite clear. The narrative demonstrates that she now lives untroubled with her wounded self-image because she knows she is intimately loved and assisted by God. She said:

I think that in becoming friends with God, there have been things that have been happening. First of all, the relationship with Jesus was established. And then there came times when I needed healing and that's where the Holy Spirit came in. That was the turning point with the Holy Spirit. The image was a cave and the doorway to the cave was a huge penny that had "In God We Trust," but that was like the stone wall of the cave. But inside was me. I had broken a wheel, a bicycle wheel, and the spokes were broken. It was kind of all bent and it was me...I was like a cavewoman, not too smart, and I was banging away and ruining my wheel and the spokes and everything. I brought Jesus to see that. Jesus looked at it and he said, "You know, you need the Holy Spirit over here." My experience of the Holy Spirit was of healing by fire and water. The *"Fons Vivus, Ignis Caritas,"* *["Living Fountain, Fiery Love"]*—that's when I began to experience the healing power of the Holy Spirit, so patient in mending the spokes on my wheel. More than once I broke it again. But again the healing came. It was as though it was a healing by searing fire but then into the fountain of water to cool. It wasn't a painful thing, but it was real. That's how the Holy Spirit got its name. At first I was only calling the Holy Spirit *Ignis* ["Fire"] but then when I saw that *Ignis* was healing over and over again, that's how come I say Faithful *Ignis* now because it's really true.

We had been asked to pray before [the thirty-day retreat] to ask what God was wanting of us at this time. Jesus said, "You be with me the whole time, just be at my side the whole time." So lots and lots of things happened in the thirty-day retreat....One of the big graces was an unburdening. God the Father came in and I was...burdened with my original sin, not knowing [how to] get out from under [it]. He said, "No daughter of mine is going to stay burdened like that for the rest of her life." Early on in the retreat there was a promise and it was fulfilled. There was an unburdening and a coming to grips with another level of understanding why this self-hatred had been gnawing away at me. There was a [personal] father connection. There was healing and forgiveness at a yet deeper level....But there was still that which I'm burdened with. There came to be a time of covenant with the Father and the Son and the Spirit. The covenant was that, yes, I know now what I'm up against, the original sin. The covenant was that they were not going to let it overcome me. I might get into the trap and I might mess things up but they were not going to let me fall through the cracks.

The next portion of her account corresponds to Ignatius's vision at La Storta.

> And then toward the end was when the friends business came. They were doing it like a corporation. They said, "We'd like you to be part of the corporation, to be part of the family. But you understand, we don't worry about salaries and promotions here." I had to go to the seminar for new people. St. Peter's the one that leads the seminar. He tells you all about it, what you do, what's expected, all that. So then with the friend idea, it's a whole other feeling and I have experienced it with my foundress and with God, that they say, "It's all right, we're glad to have this part of our work in your hands because it's just as good as if we were doing it ourselves, it's just fine...having the company in your hands. We trust you just as much as if we were doing it ourselves. So that's the kind of feeling it is."[16]

There is no heavenly court in late twenty-first-century America, but a family business corporation carries the feeling of being an insider, fully trusted with the mission. Dorothy feels entrusted by her foundress with her congregation's mission, just as she feels she is a partner with the Trinity in all that she does.

Although the above discussion uses the *Exercises* as the context for describing and illustrating the theme of mutuality with God, this theme appears throughout the mystical tradition in descriptions of the more mature stages of spiritual development. Because this is such a neglected theme in our reflection on and in our approach to spiritual direction, it is very easy to miss it or to neglect fostering its emergence. This may be all the more so for men and women whose growth toward God takes place in the midst of ordinary life or in active service to others. Spiritual directors will more easily recognize the subtle signs of the development of mutuality with God in their directees if they expect to find evidence of it. If we as directors understand that "becoming full grown in God," to use Hadewijch's phrase, entails mutuality with God, then we will recognize the subtle appearance of such mutuality in descriptions of experiences of the Spirit related to daily life and not just those related to focused times of prayer or retreat.

Teresa of Avila's Development toward Mutuality with God

To further reinforce the ubiquity of this theme in the tradition, I want to briefly share Constance FitzGerald's analysis of a similar experience of mutuality and equality with God that she discovered primarily in Teresa of Avila, but also in the teaching of John of the Cross. FitzGerald analyzes the content of Teresa's visions of Jesus, noting the changes in Teresa's self-image and her corresponding image of Jesus, until Teresa and Jesus become mirrors of one another. FitzGerald suggests that the pressures of culture and education prevent us from recognizing the equality and mutuality that Teresa's visions illustrate and that, according to John's teaching, occur in the latter stages of transformation.

John taught that God's desire is to exalt the soul and make her equal:

> If anything pleases him, it is the exaltation of the soul. Since there is no way by which he can exalt her more than by making her equal to himself, he is pleased only with her love. For the property of love is to make the lover equal to the object loved. Since the soul in this state possesses perfect love, she is called the bride of the Son of God, which signifies equality with him. In this equality of friendship the possessions of both are held in common, as the Bridegroom himself said to his disciples: I have now called you my friends, because all that I have heard from my Father I have made known to you....As a result they are truly gods by participation, equals and companions of God.[17]

The mutuality of the lover and Beloved, which is a result of mystical transformation, comprises the main theme of the middle section of the "Spiritual Canticle." Both Teresa's and John's writings include plenty of passages not marked by this equality and mutuality—images full of suffering, distance, inequality, and even misogyny. Nevertheless, many powerful passages clearly indicate that the *goal* of the spiritual journey is mutuality.

Teresa began her spiritual journey with a divided self. Her desires were focused both on God and on human love, but vacillated between her love for Jesus and her love for a variety of friends whose visits compromised her contemplative life. She experienced these as competing and distracting loves, and it took her nearly twenty years before she could integrate them into her primary relationship with Jesus. Teresa described prayer as "...nothing else than an intimate sharing between friends; it means taking time frequently to be alone with Him who we know loves us."[18] Yet, she frequently abandoned prayer lest she herself feel abandonment. Only gradually did she discover that Jesus could and would fulfill her deepest desires and gift her with human friendships in harmony with this divine-human love.

In her analysis of Teresa's visions, FitzGerald asserts that images of the "hand of Christ" show an inequality during times when Teresa's affections were divided and conflicted. In one vision, Jesus raises her up from illness and from her own failings. She discovers that Jesus does not abandon her, even though she abandoned him. In another vision, Jesus' extended hand signifies strength, power, authority, and even superiority.

> It seemed impossible, my Lord, to abandon you so completely. And since I did forsake you so many times I cannot but fear. For when you withdrew a little from me, I fell to the ground. Although I abandoned you, you did not abandon me so completely as not to turn to raise me up by always holding out your hand to me.[19]

In one of her first visions, in which she actually is simultaneously with a friend, Teresa saw a severe-looking Christ who clearly disapproved of this relationship. Only later, when Teresa's friendships no longer interfere with her contemplative life, are their hands—hers and Christ's—joined in mutuality.

Although Teresa continued to vacillate in relationships and in prayer, she saw in vision the "wounded Christ," alone, afflicted, and in need. As she contemplated the poor, suffering Christ, she began to experience God's presence, tenderness, and love gradually pervading her life. At this point, she surrendered herself into the hands of God. Her first locution confirms her conflict about her friendships. Jesus says, "No longer do I want you to converse with men but with angels."[20] The power of this locution enabled Teresa to make a decisive choice for Jesus, although not without a struggle. She gradually shifted the center of her affections to the divine presence and guidance. She reported: "...I have never again been able to tie myself to any friendship or to find consolation or bear particular love for any other persons than those I understand love Him and strive to serve Him."[21]

This growth into friendship with Jesus was long and confusing, especially since her experience of spiritual direction was not always particularly helpful. The passage below reflects the trial-by-error process through which she discovers Jesus as most truly her friend.

> O, my Lord, how you are my true friend...Oh, who will cry out for you, to tell everyone how faithful you are to Your friends! All things fail; you, Lord of all, never fail. O my God, who has the understanding, the learning and the new words with which to extol your works as my soul understands them? All fails me...but if you will not abandon me, I will not fail you.[22]

As she continued to grow in her trust and confidence in this intimate friend who so empowered her, Christ became her teacher. When the books that helped her most were put on the Index and burned by the Inquisition, she complained to Jesus, who appeared to her and promised: "I will be a living book for you."[23] She continued to feel Christ beside her and experienced deep mutuality and understanding pass between them: "The Lord puts what he wants the soul to know very deeply within it, and there he makes it known without image or explicit words....And this manner in which God gives the soul understanding of his desires, and great truths and mysteries is worthy of close attention."[24]

Despite her sense of inferiority about her lack of education, Teresa discovered that "The soul sees in an instant that it is wise," and she was filled with an inner wisdom and an inner affirmation. Jesus began to mirror Teresa; she saw herself in him and him (his wisdom) in herself. Teresa grew both more independent and at the same time more deeply bonded in affection to Jesus: "The Lord desired to show me only his hands which were so very beautiful....After a few days I saw also that divine face which it seems left me completely absorbed. Since afterwards he granted me the favor of seeing him entirely, I couldn't understand why the Lord showed himself to me...."[25]

Jesus' hands now belong to Teresa and invite her trust. They lead her according to her need (weakness). The image of the face is also very powerful. Another's loving face mirrors us, helps us see ourselves, and feel real and responded to. Later, it will be Jesus' face through which Teresa will glimpse her own sublime dignity.

Teresa went through a period of doubt and confusion because her spiritual directors resisted this development toward mutuality. However, her union with God eventually reached another level of intimacy and passion. This was expressed through the visionary imagery of the fiery angel known as the transverberation, which left her "all on fire with great love for God."[26] Teresa's desire for God was thereby deepened; this vision enlivened her love, which became boundless spiritual energy serving her unique mission. As her own heart was pierced and broken open—allowing God to claim her—she fully chose God.

As these movements unfolded over time, Teresa developed an easy familiarity with God, and her companionship with Jesus became stable. She says: "I began to talk to the Lord in a foolish way, which I often do without knowing what I am saying. It is love that is then speaking, and...the soul is so transported that I don't know the difference there is between it and God."[27] She and Jesus are becoming increasingly part of one another. As Teresa enters into intercession for and friendship with other reformers and lovers of God, she discovers her human loves as part of this one great love. She says: "I saw Christ with awesome majesty and glory showing great happiness over what was taking place. Thus he told me and wanted me to see clearly that he is always present in conversations like these and how much he is pleased when persons so delight in speaking of him."[28] She is no longer divided within herself. Her vision portrays this harmony through the face of the approving Christ.

The final vision illustrating Teresa's growth into mutuality with God is among the last she describes in the *Life*. Constance FitzGerald says: "There is no vision in the whole of Teresa's writings that thrills me like this imagery."[29] She has become a perfect reflection, a mirror of Christ. The Christ-image is now fully formed in her own soul:

> [My soul] seemed to me to be like a brightly polished mirror, without any part on the back or sides or top or bottom that wasn't totally clear. In its center Christ our Lord was shown to

me....It seemed to me I saw him clearly in every part of my soul, as though in a mirror. And this mirror also...was completely engraved upon the Lord himself by means of a loving communication I wouldn't know how to describe.[30]

Together these passages clearly show how Teresa's self-image and her Christ-image correlate with one another throughout her spiritual development. They also clearly reveal the goal or term of the spiritual journey as Teresa understood it. Each of us is to be "placed with Christ," as Ignatius was, or to experience that same intimacy and mutuality that Teresa describes in her images of friendship, faces, hands, and mirrors, leading finally to the sharing of all in spiritual marriage.[31]

Even these brief allusions to a few major mystics in the Christian tradition indicate the importance and pervasiveness of mutuality with God as a feature of mature spiritual life. At the same time, most of us have neither recognized this to be so nor expect it in our spiritual direction. Although this has been a neglected theme, changes in our sense of our selves as well as in our images of God make it far more common in contemporary experience.

Many spiritual directors hold that only a very, very few approach the latter stages of mystical development. While the number doing so is, most likely, relatively small within the general population of ordinary believers, I do not think this development is particularly rare among men and women who have seriously committed themselves to God and to the practice of prayer. Those who seek spiritual direction consistently for many years are the most likely group to experience this development. Hopefully, the rather extended and detailed discussion of this theme creates new possibilities for spiritual directors. By recognizing and supporting the emergence of mutuality with God, directors can be more helpful in assisting directees in whom this mutuality is beginning to develop.

This chapter has included examples from the experience of both men and women. Examples such as Ignatius's vision at La Storta, William's sense of the centrality of love, the reciprocal bathing in Dorothy's retreat narrative, or Hadewijch's bold statement about "that luxuriant land where Beloved and loved one shall wholly flow through each other" concretely illustrate gendered versions of mutuality with God as they occur in peoples' lives. As directors, what difference might it make if, as we companion people in their prayer experiences, we evoked such possibilities by the language we used and the experiences we affirmed?

FOR FURTHER REFLECTION:[32]

- What are the other images of mutuality with God/Jesus that have emerged in your experience or in that of your directees?
- If you paid more attention to this theme in your prayer or in your directees' accounts of their experience, what might be the results and how do you feel about them?
- What are the relational equivalents of mutuality with God for you?
- Do images from nature expand your sense of who God might be?
- Are you free to allow these images to emerge spontaneously in your directees' experience and to explore them together, giving them rapt attention, allowing them to expand?

- Are you alert as a director to the correlative self-/God-images implied by your directees' descriptions?
- What corrective spiritual exercises might heal images of God that inhibit this development of intimacy and mutuality?

NOTES

1. *Hadewijch: The Complete Works*, trans. Mother Columba Hart. Classics of Western Spirituality (Mahwah, N.J.: Paulist Press, 1980), "Poems in Stanzas," poem 4, l. 47.

2. See Elisabeth Schüssler Fiorenza, *In Memory of Her* (New York: Crossroad, 1983).

3. The September/October 1998 issue of the *Utne Reader* focused on these new gender studies, which suggest that gender is distinct from sex and is a social construction far more fluid than many of us imagine.

4. In this discussion of gender assumption, I am not making statements about individual men or women personally, but about the conventional arrangements in Western society at the present time. Individuals vary considerably in their consciousness of and choices related to sexism, inclusive language, and gender assumptions as they play out in the God-human relationship.

5. I am indebted here to my colleague, Dr. John J. Shea, O.S.A., and his developmental theory of masculinity and spirituality, which was presented in the workshop we developed together at Fordham University: "Differing Journeys: Masculine and Feminine Spirituality."

6. See Elizabeth Johnson's "Mary and the Female Face of God" in *Theological Studies* 50 (1989): 500–26 and *She Who Is: The Mystery of God in Feminist Theological Discourse* (New York: Crossroad, 1992).

7. John Giles Milhaven. *Hadewijch and Her Sisters: Other Ways of Loving and Knowing* (Albany: State University of New York Press, 1993) and Constance FitzGerald, O.C.D., "A Discipleship of Equals: Voices from Tradition—Teresa of Avila and John of the Cross," in *A*

Discipleship of Equals: Towards a Christian Feminist Spirituality, ed. Francis A. Eigo (Villanova: Villanova University Press, 1988), 63–97.

8. *The Spiritual Exercises of St. Ignatius*, trans. Louis J. Puhl, S.J. (Chicago: Loyola University Press, 1951), nos. 230–37.

9. Ibid., no. 230.1.

10. Ibid., no. 231.2.

11. Ibid., no. 234.

12. *Hadewijch*, "Poems in Stanzas," poem 4, ll. 43–48; cf. poems 35 and 36 and letter 6, no. 350 ff.

13. Sue Woodruff, *Meditations with Mechthild of Magdeburg* (Santa Fe: Bear and Company, 1982), 79.

14. Ibid., 88.

15. Ibid., 89.

16. Interview material used with permission.

17. "Spiritual Canticle," 28.1, in *The Collected Works of St. John of the Cross*, trans. Kieran Kavanaugh and Otilio Rodriquez (Washington, D.C.: Institute of Carmelite Studies, 1973).

18. *Life*, 8.5. in *The Collected Works of Teresa of Avila*, trans. Kieran Kavanaugh and Otilio Rodriquez, 3 vols. (Washington, D.C.: Institute of Carmelite Studies, 1976–85).

19. Ibid., 7.1.

20. Ibid., 24.5.

21. Ibid., 24.6.

22. Ibid., 25.17–19.

23. Ibid., 26.5.

24. Ibid., 27.6.

25. Ibid., 28.1.

26. Ibid., 29.10.

27. Ibid., 34.8,3.

28. Ibid., 34.17.

29. FitzGerald, "A Discipleship of Equals," 83. I am indebted to Constance FitzGerald's splendid analysis of this theme throughout the entire section.

30. *Life*, 40.5.

31. Ironically, Teresa's experience of spiritual marriage occurred while the book of her *Life* was in the hands of the inquisitors.

32. Some of these questions were suggested by Andrew J. Dufner's reflection on the initial version of this chapter at the Ignatian Spirituality Institute, August 10, 1995.

Chapter 6

THE "AS IF" RELATIONSHIP: TRANSFERENCE AND COUNTERTRANSFERENCE IN SPIRITUAL DIRECTION

Spiritual directors have made a number of different assumptions about how transference and countertransference function within the spiritual direction relationship. Transference is a particular type of unconscious projection (which will be more fully described below); an awareness of the unconscious process of transference emerges from psychoanalytic schools of psychology. In psychoanalysis, the dual phenomenon of transference and countertransference is the focus of analysis and insight in the therapeutic relationship. Hence, the therapist is alert to recognize transference as it occurs and to focus directly on it in the process of therapy. Working directly with these powerful, unconscious responses requires extensive training and ongoing supervision.

Because spiritual direction focuses specifically on the directees' relationship with God—rather than on the relationship between director and directee—spiritual directors avoid engaging the transference directly. Many spiritual directors even assume that transference either does not occur or does not play a significant role in direction. There are two reasons for this: Typically, one would meet less frequently with a spiritual director than with a therapist or counselor (typically every three to four weeks rather than weekly or even more often, as in therapy).[1] Spiritual directors today differ in their opinions about whether or not this phenomenon occurs in the director-directee relationship. This raises the further question regarding how, given their level of training, individual directors might intentionally work with these dynamics in their spiritual direction sessions.

This chapter will offer some definitions and descriptions of transference and countertransference, explore the relationship between recognizing these dynamics and understanding their corresponding ethical implications, identify transferences specific to spiritual direction, and recommend some ways spiritual directors might respond to directee's transferences. The material will most likely be of greater interest to spiritual directors, but some directees might find it helpful for reflecting on confusing experiences that may have occurred in one or another spiritual direction relationship.

Transference

So, what is transference? There are two forms of it, depending on how different clinicians define it. Parataxic distortion, a mild version of transference, is projection based on predetermined patterns of relating and is an aspect of all human relationships. Transference as understood in the clinical sense, however, develops over time in a relationship when one person responds to the other "as if" the other actually were the person's parent or someone else from the distant past. Both dynamics occur regularly in spiritual direction.

The "As If" Relationship

Parataxic Distortion

Psychoanalyst Harry Stack Sullivan developed the term *parataxic distortion* to indicate that all of us contribute to some form of distortion in our relationships. Projection and distortion are not restricted to the therapeutic context alone. Psychiatrist Gerald May defines parataxic distortion as "predetermined patterns of relating to people who have certain characteristics."[2] For example, many of us have reactions to persons who are fat or tall, handicapped, male or female and so on based on our prior experience. May treats this kind of distortion as a form of prejudice, triggered by a person's external attributes that evoke memories and attitudes from previous experiences. All relationships, including the spiritual direction relationship, are susceptible to such distortion.

A very common experience of parataxic distortion occurs when we meet someone who initially reminds us in an uncanny way of someone else we have known. Usually, we become aware of such reactions fairly rapidly and can monitor them until we get to know the new person. This awareness can prevent us from acting as if he or she is the other person. As we get more familiar with the individual's uniqueness and history, the distortion usually dissolves on its own.

In spiritual direction, such distortions often occur in initial interviews. First impressions of each other may either help or hinder the relationship. If the directee has had prior experience of spiritual direction, it is often very helpful for the director to find out something about it. The directee likely brings a set of expectations, feelings, and attitudes based on their prior experience of spiritual directors. If your directee acts "as if" you are another director, you will begin to feel this type of transference. Your failure to fit the expectation will reveal the distortion going on in the directee. These expectations are often revealed by body language, the way the directee looks at you (or doesn't), deferential expressions, idealistic projections, or offhand comments such as "you probably think I'm silly, foolish, crazy, bad, etcetera," when you are thinking nothing of the kind. As a director, being "real," being yourself, or being as genuine as possible with a directee helps minimize these responses when and as they occur.

Conversely, directors may make the same kinds of false assumptions about directees who fit particular profiles. A new directee's appearance, state of life, occupation, gender, age, ethnic background, sexual orientation, size, physical disability or illness, or special gifts may all evoke stereotypical responses from the director based on past experience or prejudice. It is, perhaps, most helpful to assume we know nothing about directees until they disclose themselves to us. Listening to the unique aspects of a directee's story helps dissipate a mindset based on prior experience and allows the director to meet the directee as he or she actually is.

Transference

According to psychiatrist and spiritual director Gerald May, "transference refers to specific situations in psychotherapy in which a patient unconsciously invests the therapist with qualities and attributes pertaining to the patient's mother, father, or some other person of childhood significance and then proceeds to act *as if* the therapist really were that person."[3] As with the more mild parataxic distortion, sustained incidences of transference do occur in the spiritual direction relationship. A directee's transference, which happens gradually during the course of spiritual direction, is simply the result of previous relationships with authority figures, usually parents.

Anyone is susceptible to bringing unresolved emotional conflicts to the spiritual direction relationship and reenacting them in this new setting. Whenever directees are preoccupied with what their directors think or feel about them and base their self-presentations and self-disclosures on such perceptions, transference is going on. The directee begins to act "as if" the director is someone from the past. A simple example may help.

> A young, gay male directee develops a relationship with another retreatant while on retreat. Both men see the same director for retreat interviews. One directee talks about this developing relationship and its significance in the context of his religious experience; the other avoids all mention of it as he shares about his prayer. The director begins to feel the second directee is being evasive, maybe even consciously deceptive. This directee's narration lacks energy and concreteness with the result that the prayer dynamics somehow seem superficial or disconnected from the directee. When the director questions this directee about what might be happening, he says, "Well, I haven't exactly had a very good track record with spiritual directors whenever I tried to bring my gay relationships into the conversation." The directee then goes on to recount two very negative experiences with other experienced directors while on retreat.

Both directees know and trust the director. Because of their experiences (with other directors and as well as with this one), however, they anticipate very different responses from her. They "transfer" their positive and negative expectations respectively. The first directee expects the director to receive this experience nonjudgmentally and to accompany him through the process of the relationship in the retreat context. The second, carrying wounds from authority in the past, is self-protective and unable to entrust his experience to the director until she invites it. The negative transference affects the director enough for her to wonder, "What is going on? Why do I feel unable to connect with the second man's experience?" The positive transference of the first directee indicates to the director that it is most likely not her personal response to these directees that accounts for the difference in their willingness to entrust their experience to her. If she were unconsciously homophobic, most likely neither directee would offer the experience.

This example might elicit any number of emotional reactions from directors. In the case of the second directee, unresolved issues about his homosexual orientation and relationships could evoke everything from approval to moral condemnation. His issues could also bring forth feelings of empathy, compassion, identification, or even sexual interest. For another director, the fact that these two men are spending a significant amount of time on a silent retreat talking with and relating to one another instead of placing their primary relational focus on their relationship with God could evoke anger, disapproval, disappointment, and so forth. What responses from a retreat director to this situation and to each of these directees would facilitate the retreat process for both men and enhance their growth and development?

Countertransference

In order to discuss this complex example further, it is necessary to define and describe countertransference. In spiritual direction, countertransference refers to a director's transference reactions to the directee. According to psychologist and professor Robert Wicks, countertransference "is an unrealistic response to a person's realistic behavior, transferences, and general relationship with the helper and the world. Countertransferences are primarily based on the *helper's* past significant relationships; basically they gratify his or her needs rather than the...directee's."[4] Wicks's description suggests that countertransference includes an element of exaggeration or distortion and is unrealistic, usually meaning that there is an unconscious aspect to the response.

Countertransference, furthermore, is elicited by the directee and is reciprocal.[5] Just as our self-image and our image of God is correlative, so too, is the transference/countertransference response. The directee requires the director to enact the role that corresponds to the initial transference. If the directee acts childlike, for instance, he or she will elicit a parental response of some kind. If directees flatter us, they may wish us to return the flattery, which makes it very difficult to discover and engage their negative qualities. If we respond unreflectively to our directees' unconscious expectations of us, we will most likely be serving our own needs rather than our directees'.

In the example above, the director felt the second directee's transferential fear. If the director had allowed that wariness to prevent her from questioning or exploring what was happening from the directee's point of view, she may have gotten caught in the countertransference. She may have accumulated too much suspicion or anger to have been helpful to her directee and inhibited the directee's ability to self-disclose at all. When she wondered with the directee about what the most important events in the retreat were, the directee expressed not only his previous negative experiences with other directors but also included a comment revealing a deeper problem with authority. He said something like, "My previous experience with directors with good reputations were so disastrous, do you think I would bring my homosexual issues to you? After all, you are an authority on spiritual direction!" This comment revealed to the director the discrepancy between how she perceived her own authority and the exaggerated degree of authority her directee conferred on her. With that awareness, the director avoided a response based on the feelings the directee elicited and instead referred the directee back to his own experience, his own authority, his ongoing relationship with God. Suddenly, the directee was fully in the retreat process again.[6] He was no longer acting "as if" his director were one of the authorities with which he had difficulty.

Psychologist and professor Michael Cavanaugh says, in the context of the counseling relationship, that "all transference reactions have a quality of resistance. As long as people are spending time and energy loving or hating the counselor, they are not progressing toward the mutually agreed upon goals."[7] This is also true of spiritual direction. When the relationship between the director and directee—instead of the directee's relationship with God—becomes the focus of the direction conversation or a preoccupation for the directee, the entire process of spiritual direction can be sidetracked. While spiritual directors need to be aware of transferential phenomena in their directees and in themselves, they also need to remember that neither all reactions of the directee nor all conflicts that may arise are transference. Many reactions and conflicts are entirely reality-based—our mistakes or successes evoke appropriately negative or positive reactions.

Reasons Directors Miss Transferential Phenomenon

My experience of supervising intern spiritual directors for the last fifteen years has heightened my awareness of how failing to attend to transferential reactions in spiritual directors can harm directees. Beginning spiritual directors, precisely because of their inexperience, can easily fail to recognize their professional responsibility toward directees. These failures may occur for three reasons: adherence to a spiritual friendship model of spiritual direction; inadequate awareness of the power differential in the relationship; and a lack of the skills required to recognize and manage transference and countertransference.

Spiritual Friendship Model of Direction

Spiritual directors who advocate a spiritual friendship model of direction may dramatically underestimate the level of responsibility a spiritual director assumes in this sacred relationship. Although there are, in fact, precious instances of fully mutual spiritual friendships in Christian tradition, they remain relatively rare. Even though it bears a resemblance to spiritual friendship, spiritual direction by its very nature is usually not an entirely mutual or equal relationship.[8] Spiritual direction relationships entail an implied or explicit covenant to serve the spiritual well-being of the person seeking spiritual direction. Thus, it constitutes a pastoral relationship, requiring the spiritual director to assume ethical responsibility for this pastoral ministry.

Lack of Awareness of the Power Differential

Several recent writers address such ethical responsibilities on the basis of the power differential in the relationship.[9] Psychologist Donna Markham and therapist Fran Repka identify numerous sources of emotional vulnerability within pastoral relationships.[10] By virtue of the difference in role between directees and their spiritual directors, directees are more vulnerable. They reveal intimate details about their lives and religious experiences to their directors. The directors, however, do not engage in the same level of self-disclosure.

Other sources of power differences include the relative balance of resources. In this relationship, who has the greater knowledge and experience of the spiritual life? Who in the relationship is burdened by poverty and oppression? Who in the relationship is in a period of pain, weakness, or crisis? Who in the relationship has the greater social resources of support, community, and family? Who in the relationship has the greater physical resources in terms of health, ability, size, or strength? This list, of course, is not exhaustive. Sometimes, too, the spiritual director may be the more vulnerable in one area of life, rendering him or her more susceptible to abusing power in the relationship because of personal neediness.

Whenever an emotionally vulnerable person entrusts him- or herself to an identified ministerial person, the latter is ethically responsible for maintaining appropriate boundaries and for preventing harm to the more vulnerable person. Boundary transgressions often occur because the pastoral person fails to recognize and reflect on how the more vulnerable person's transference is affecting him or her. The power differential in ministerial relationships can best be respected through awareness of transference and countertransference. Our ethical responsibility as spiritual directors includes managing transference.

Skills Required to Manage Transference

Managing transference and countertransference requires highly developed interpersonal skills. Awareness of transferential reactions is based on a spiritual directors' abilities to recognize the feelings evoked in them by directees and to make judgments about whether or not—and how—they are going to act on the basis of that information.

Neophyte spiritual directors are usually not able to process their directees' manifest content fast enough to also track the subliminal communication going on in the transference. Usually, an experienced supervisor is more skillful at surfacing useful information, which is available in the reciprocal response evoked in the director. In the supervisory session, directors are free to explore and express their feelings and discover how they might use this information to explore issues raised by their directees. Directly engaging and interpreting directees' transferences usually requires professional training in counseling. Through supervision and psychological consultation, spiritual directors can learn to manage the transference and use information derived from it in ways appropriate to spiritual direction and their own individual levels of professional training.

Initial Awareness of Positive and Negative Transference

Positive Transference

We can now offer some general recommendations for dealing with transference, especially emotionally positive forms of transference such as respect, esteem, appreciation, gratitude, and idealization of the spiritual director. Positive transference usually makes the director feel good, worthwhile, and relatively competent as a director and enables the director to develop a positive working alliance with the directee. Most psychologists recommend, even in the counseling situation, that mild to moderate positive transference be noticed and basically ignored. From this position of positive connection, the director can gradually earn their directees' trust and remain focused on their directees' relationship with God.

Exaggerated positive transference is considerably more uncomfortable for spiritual directors, especially less experienced directors, to receive. The expressions of admiration and praise are so unrealistic that directors receiving these projections become extremely anxious because they know they cannot live up to such expectations. Sometimes, directors will deliberately make mistakes to prove they are not as good as the directee wants to believe. Frequently, directors will immediately begin to engage the transference in order to reduce their own anxiety. Since engaging the transference in this case is in the director's interest—meeting the director's need, rather than the directee's—this type of transference is best left alone within the context of the direction relationship itself.

In the case of exaggerated positive transference, directors can more fruitfully express their anxiety and discomfort in supervision. By recognizing the strength of the transference, they can gain perspective through a healthy sense of humor and by not taking these projections as evidence of their own superior gifts! Directors can also probe the feelings experienced with such directees and notice how they might be inhibiting exploration of the directees' experiences: Is the directee's need to exalt the director a means of avoiding something the directee doesn't want the director to discover? Usually, after a supervision session, the spiritual director regains confidence and feels less self-conscious and more natural in the spiritual director role. This normalcy of relational response helps directees to withdraw their unrealistic projections.

Negative Transference

Mild to Moderate Negative Transference

A second variety of transference, which can be handled in a similar fashion, is unexpressed mild to moderate negative transference on the part of the directee. The gay directee mentioned above, who was not disclosing part of his experience in the retreat, provides an example. In this instance, the negative projection was based upon fear of an authority. Other negative feelings directees may project are anger, aggressiveness, jealousy, and competitiveness.

The "As If" Relationship

Directors may become anxious when they begin to sense these unexpressed feelings and to perceive their own feelings and responses in return. By talking about them in supervision, however, directors can learn skills that enable them to resist letting such feelings restrict their freedom in spiritual direction sessions. It is clear that this process of subsequent reflection renders the spiritual director vulnerable with a supervisor, which frequently results in an expanded self-knowledge and challenges him or her to personal and professional growth. If appropriate, a competent supervisor will help the director by identifying further means of completing the director's personal work, proposing specific spiritual exercises or forms of prayer, suggesting content to explore with the director's spiritual director, and, perhaps, indicating a need for growth-oriented therapeutic work.

A far more challenging situation than a directee's mild negative transference is a director's recognition of negative feelings toward particular directees. This may happen in situations, such as in retreat houses, where directees are assigned to a retreat director. If these negative responses are based on first impressions, which are fairly superficial, they dissipate rather quickly as the director begins to actually relate to the directee. Even greater challenges arise, however, if the director's negative feelings toward the directee do not dissipate in the first couple of sessions. If these negative feelings are evoked by the directee's expressed transferential anger, hatred, jealousy, or such, the spiritual director should respond to these feelings as nondefensively as possible. Such experiences are unpleasant and also unnerving for a spiritual director. Sometimes, simply expressing these feelings in supervision can reduce this threat to a director's composure and confidence.

Strong Negative Transference Usually Requires Supervision

If a directee evokes strong, negative, initial feelings in a director—presuming that the director in question rarely experiences such reactions from others and, more importantly, has not responded so poorly to a directee that negative responses are genuinely deserved—it may indicate the directee needs in-depth therapy. In supervision the director might discuss whether to refer the directee to someone else, either a trained therapist or a pastoral counselor who may be more skilled in working with such transference. Ordinarily, a spiritual director would have to be professionally trained as a counselor as well as a spiritual director to manage strong, negative, persistent transference successfully in spiritual direction. It is very challenging for a director to work with someone with whom he or she cannot make a positive connection. If a director is struggling hard to control negative responses to the directee, it is likely the director will end up harming the directee.

Although spiritual directors do not try to foster transference, these dynamics are simply a part of the helping relationship. The more frequent the sessions, the longer the relationship, and the more opaque the director, the more likely it is that significant transference will develop. This explains why spiritual directors need to participate in some form of supervision. Individual or group supervision helps directors maintain their self-awareness and minimize countertransference reactions.

Group supervision tends to benefit all of the group members. When spiritual directors reflect with one another on their work, they all profit from the cases presented, some of which may remind participants of similar experiences with their own directees. Learning from others' experiences brings transferential material to consciousness in a helpful way. Assisting spiritual directors in recognizing transference and responding to it appropriately and constructively is one of the primary reasons for supervision. Reflection on the director's countertransference often provides a clue to something in the directee as well as to something happening in the director. If directors are unaware of responding in overly positive or overly negative ways to their directees, they can easily become confused by the transference and serve their directees less effectively.

Because of the nature of spiritual direction, supervision is not merely a psychological process, but a spiritual one as well. Directors are profoundly affected by directees. We need to assimilate and reflect on the way God touches us and acts upon us through directees as well as on how we respond to those invitations of grace. We also need to pay attention to how God moves and graces us in the process of direction itself. We need to be supple in God's hands, sufficiently free to be at the service of the directee, and available to God's guidance in our sessions. Attending to the transference and countertransference in our direction sessions increases our self-knowledge and invites us to greater psychological growth. In a similar way, attending to the ways our directees affect us spiritually leads us toward continued development in this area.

Transferences Specific to Spiritual Direction Relationship

With a general understanding of the dynamics of transference and countertransference, we can now identify and explore some transferences likely to arise because of the nature of the spiritual direction relationship itself. These include four distinct yet overlapping possibilities.

- Directees frequently idealize their directors because they embody or symbolize spiritual qualities to which directees aspire.

- Directees may unconsciously conflate God and their spiritual directors.
- Directees may develop a special attachment to their directors related to their soul-friendship.
- Directees may identify their directors with a particular religious institution, such as their denomination, their religious order, their local congregation, etcetera.

Idealization of the Spiritual Director

The spiritual director often embodies a spiritual model to which the directee aspires. Because spiritual directors often fulfill another public pastoral role, this transference can be complex and include other features a particular director is perceived to embody. Directees may perceive their directors to be prayerful, contemplative, peaceful, loving, wise, or a model of spiritual authority (a teacher, leader, or director). They see in their directors the people they might want to become or, in fact, already are becoming.

Many of us who are spiritual directors recognize we learned a great deal about becoming a spiritual director through our experience as directees. We learned what helpful or harmful spiritual direction felt like. When we became spiritual directors, we had to discover how God worked through our unique personalities for the good of others. We discovered we had to embody the qualities and behaviors we admired in our directors in our own way.

Spiritual directors need to keep two things in mind when directees idealize us. First, as with the positive projections discussed above, we need to guard against inflation. We need to recognize that we are not necessarily as wonderful as our directees make us feel. We need to notice the projection, recognize the element of truth in it, and not take the exaggeration too seriously. It is also important to maintain our personal integrity and professional responsibility in the relationship. If we begin to believe the flattery of our directees, we may more easily become careless about boundary issues.

Secondly, once we've identified the qualities projected onto us, we can, in response to our directees, helpfully encourage them to embody these qualities themselves. If we reflect back to them the "ideal" they see in us as something that is very important to them and that they may already be developing, they become free to withdraw the projection without necessarily discussing it as a projection. In this process, the focus remains on the directees and their hopes, ideals, and desires—helping them recognize that this is something to which they aspire.

Spiritual Directors Symbolically Represent God

Spiritual directors become intimately associated in their directees' thoughts, feelings, and memories of their experience of God. As spiritual confidants, directors receive and share many of their directees' most significant life experiences. Through the directors' attentive and loving acceptance of their directees' religious experience, they become an important mediation of religious experience. When directors help their directees respond to God's initiatives and deepen their relationship with God, directees usually express gratitude. Directors often offer their directees a loving acceptance that eventually helps them receive even more satisfying love and acceptance directly from God. As a consequence, directees sometimes weave the director right into their relationship with God.

Whether we like it or not and whether we are comfortable with it or not, we as directors receive a transference from directees that rightfully belongs to God. This constitutes more than an ordinary authority projection, although that, too, will be going on and will give us some hints about whether that authority projection will impede or enhance a directee's relationship with God. This direct association of the director with God is more delicate than that. Directors need to be able to tolerate it comfortably without fostering it or being seduced into taking God's place in the directee's life.

The way we as directors respond to directees' material often images for them how God might be interested in that aspect of their lives and might respond to it. Frequently, an intense mirroring process takes place, and this is a normal part of spiritual direction. As directees share their lives with us they are becoming more aware of themselves, their feelings, and their ability to enter into the kind of God-human intimacy described in the previous chapter. The director who wondered with Diane about Jesus' need to be ministered to made such an intervention. After receiving what Diane already recognized as a very important experience, the director gently invited her to focus her attention right back on Jesus. Her contemplation unfolded in the scene of mutual bathing.

This mirroring of God for our directees can take either a positive or a negative form. Our reactions either facilitate or hinder our directees' relationship with God. A high level of presence, empathy, unconditional love, challenge, respect, and so forth, usually facilitates our directees' experience of God. Our failing to manifest these qualities or communicating anxiety, anger, judgment, or rigidity to directees may hinder their relationship with God. Although we never put ourselves in the place of God, we become deeply associated with God. That means we must be particularly reverent and respectful of the sacred trust of our directees and constantly help them shift their primary focus away from their relationship with us and toward their primary relationship with God. Another example may help illustrate this process.

The "As If" Relationship

A religious man reveals in a spiritual direction session that his request to make final vows has been postponed. He is quite upset and feels hurt and rejected. He wonders about leaving his community altogether, although he recognizes that this would be adding to his sense of loss as he really enjoys the members of his community and his religious way of life. By diligent and patient listening the director draws near to the man's experience and seeks to understand his loss. At the same time the director helps facilitate the process whereby the directee may experience God's encouragement and affirmation, i.e., God's attunement. By embodying the attunement of God the director serves to enhance the directee's experience of God...who understands and empathizes. The directee may through such a process experience renewed hope.... [11]

Should a director become frightened of this God-transference, he or she may be tempted to abandon a directee through inappropriate termination. The loss of a director who had helped him or her experience God in such a positive way can present a serious obstacle to the directee's spiritual growth. The feelings of loss and anger evoked by the director's termination of the relationship can make it difficult for the directee to pray. The directee has become used to sharing these intimate experiences of God with the director and not being able to share the prayer experience can evoke grief. Some directees will then develop resistance to prayer (as discussed in chapter 2) in order to avoid these unpleasant feelings.

The delicacy of this aspect of transference in the spiritual direction relationship helps us, as directors, to recognize our importance to our directees' very connection with God. Should we need to end our relationship with them for an entirely appropriate reason, they may suffer the loss of some aspect of their relationship with God for a while. If we refer, move, or otherwise must separate from a directee, it will take a few sessions to bring closure and help the directee make a transition. In the process, we need to reinforce the fact that their primary relationship with God can and will continue without us.

Some general recommendations may be helpful for coping with the intensity of these projections from our directees. Whenever possible, we should gently point the directee toward God, so that God can console, comfort, challenge, and love them in their prayer experience in a way similar to ours and, of course, better than ours.

As directors we can use the projections we receive as clues for exploring how our directees image God and can explore the experiences in which such projections may be rooted. We are as likely to receive negative projections that suggest God may be harsh or punitive for a particular directee as we are to receive the positive attributes. Tentatively reflecting the projection back in the form of a question may enable the directee to repair an inadequate image of God by becoming conscious of the negative one. For instance, a director might say, "Sometimes I get the impression that you expect God to punish you harshly. Is that the kind of person you think God is?"

We always need to hold the sacred trust of the spiritual director role carefully. Turning to God explicitly in direction sessions allows God to hold us, so we will not become overly anxious in the face of such projections. Turning to God in this way consciously evokes a felt sense of partnership with God, so that we do not become confused by the transference, but rely on God to inspire us, assist us, and ultimately remain God for both us and our directees.

Soul Friendship with a Director Displaced as Erotic Attraction

In chapter 4 we explicitly focused on love mysticism and on the possibility that directors may become anxious and uncomfortable when they hear about explicitly erotic mystical experiences of directees or about their interpersonal sexual lives. Because we live in a sex-saturated culture that is only quite recently recognizing any form of sacred sexuality, directors may misinterpret conversation about erotic experience as the manifestation of a sexual attraction within the direction session. Sexuality is an aspect of every relationship. And an erotic transference will elicit some kind of response in directors. With recent sexual misconduct a publicly acknowledged fact of ministerial life, it is important to carefully monitor our reactions and attractions as directors and not sexualize a spiritual direction relationship. To do so egregiously harms directees precisely because of our association with the religious dimension of their lives.[12]

Chapter 4 explored the relationship between human love and sexuality and divine-human intimacy trying to happen. Both directees and directors are susceptible to missing the divine aim of human desiring even in quite problematic sexual relationships. It is also not uncommon, as Gerald May so wisely pointed out, that the upsurge of pure love in contemplative experience is easily displaced into a human relationship. This often occurs because directees do not yet know how to recognize that the source of this pure love is God and that the love should be focused on God.[13]

There is, however, a less well-understood kind of attraction between directors and directees. A director can become particularly anxious upon discovering that a directee has fallen in love with the director's soul and has come to love God in and through the director's intimacy with God. Directors can easily confuse this attraction with romantic love; they need to learn to recognize this attraction as transference without responding inappropriately.

In this case, the directee may be learning from the director's way of being with God and with the directee. The attraction is rooted in the spiritual dimension, and happens through a kind of spiritual affinity. In Sufism, for example, spiritual guides are chosen through such spiritual attraction or attunement. If a director has been very instrumental in the directee's spiritual growth, the attraction may be even stronger due to the director's close association with God and the directee's experience of God. This is not a new experience. Teresa of Avila responded to such concerns in *The Way of Perfection*, where she counsels her sisters that it is normal to develop an attraction for a confessor. She matter-of-factly asserts that we will love those who have been helpful to our souls and suggests that one should not be unduly concerned about it.

Nevertheless, if the director misinterprets this attraction for erotic desire and rejects the directee or creates distance in direction sessions, great harm can be done to the directee's spiritual life. Most of the time it is enough for the director to recognize the particular quality of this transference for what it is and not disturb the directee. The same guidelines apply in this case as were discussed in other instances of positive transference.

In addition, it is the director's responsibility to maintain necessary boundaries and to receive this particular form of love without confusing it with others. Spiritual attractions can be mutually very alluring. Great maturity is needed in both persons to find mutuality of expression, as some rare persons historically have and continue to do. There exists a mutuality of grace and of inspiration, although usually only one side is expressed in the spiritual direction relationship. With such mature directees, it can be helpful to recognize and affirm the kind of love particular to this relationship. Above all, both should consciously resist attempts to romanticize or eroticize the relationship.

The "As If" Relationship

Spiritual Directors Receive Institutional Transference

Like other pastoral ministers, spiritual directors stand for particular religious institutions, such as an entire denomination, the local church, religious life, clergy, or some other organization related to religion or spirituality.[14] Most directees will approach spiritual directors with the reverence they offer most religious professionals. Although all spiritual directors may not be closely associated with their churches in other official ministerial roles, most directees will transfer some aspects of institutional expectations to them. This transference can evoke an automatic response from directors, rapidly moving them out of the spiritual direction role and into another, such as preaching, teaching, administering the sacraments, and so forth. Spiritual direction may be a privileged place for some directees to develop an adult self and faith in relationship to religious institutions. In these cases, spiritual directors need to recognize the transference and invite directees to make adult decisions and faith commitments based on religious experience and critical reflection.

Spiritual directors may fruitfully notice and process their comfort or discomfort with these projections in supervision. It remains challenging to most directors to free ourselves from feeling too responsible for our directees and at the same time assume responsibility for working with our own countertransferences when we touch on common institutional areas.

In this chapter we have explored the reciprocal phenomenon of the "as if" relationship, technically known as transference and countertransference. This experience exists in any helping relationship. Although spiritual directors are not necessarily clinically trained to interpret or analyze transference, we do need to have a basic understanding of transference in general and how it evokes a variety of responses in us. Learning to recognize some aspects of transferential reactions through the process of supervision can enhance our ability as directors to maintain the focus on our directees' relationship with God without becoming confused or irresponsible in our responses to our directees. Reflecting on the quality and feelings in the transference can help us better understand how our directees may be perceiving and relating to God as well as to us. There is much to be learned from the many facets of the "as if" relationship specific to the spiritual direction relationship.

FOR FURTHER REFLECTION:

- Which directees in particular come to mind as you reflect on the "as if" relationship?
- What unexpressed feelings do you sense they might have toward you or toward something you might represent?
- How might you use this awareness as a guide to areas you might wish to explore with your directee?
- What feelings do you have when you are with this directee? Are they different from the way you usually feel with other directees or is there something unique (for you) in your feelings, behaviors, or preoccupations with this directee? Try to describe, as concretely as possible, a "typical" kind of interchange or pattern in your sessions with the directee.
- Were there any "aha" moments while reading this chapter? What were they? What do you feel might be going on for you either as a director or directee?
- In a supervisory session you might consider role-playing a directee. Your supervisor or peers may be able to

identify your directee's feelings and projections toward you and reflect them back to you.

NOTES

1. See Gerald May, *Care of Mind/Care of Spirit* (San Francisco: Harper, 1992), ch. 6, 103 ff. and William Barry and William Connolly, *The Practice of Spiritual Direction* (Mahwah, N.J.: Paulist Press, 1982), ch. 10, for such discussions.

2. May, *Care of Mind/Care of Spirit*, 126.

3. Ibid.

4. Robert Wicks, "Countertransference in Spiritual Direction" in *Human Development* 6 (Fall 1985): 13.

5. I am indebted to a practicum presentation by Dr. Beverly Musgrave, in the spring of 1999 at Fordham University, for this insight about transference.

6. In "A Psychiatrist's View of Transference and Countertransference in the Pastoral Relationship" (*The Journal of Pastoral Care* [Spring 1989]: 41 ff.), Richard S. Schwartz claims the literature on countertransference includes three meanings: the director's transference to the directee, the director's unconscious response to the directee's transference, and all the director's emotional responses to the directee. According to Schwartz, including all of the pastoral ministers' responses makes the definition too broad to be helpful. However, I maintain that all three of these responses are important material for directors to explore in either individual or group supervision in order to learn when and how to use this important emotional information for the benefit of one's directees.

7. Michael E. Cavanaugh, *The Counseling Experience: A Theoretical and Practical Approach* (Monterey: Brooks/Cole, 1982), 130 ff.

8. See my "Spiritual Direction: An Instance of Christian Friendship or a Therapeutic Relationship?" in *Studia Mystica* 12 (Spring 1989): 64–73.

9. See Richard M. Gula, *Ethics in Pastoral Ministry* (Mahwah, N.J.: Paulist Press, 1996) for a most helpful discussion of these issues. See also Paul B. Macke, "Boundaries in Ministerial Relationships" in *Human Development* 14 (Spring 1993): 23–25.

10. Donna J. Markham and Fran Repka, "Personal Development and Boundaries Shape Ministry" in *Human Development* (Spring 1997): 33–45.

11. C. Kevin Gillespie, "Listening for Grace: Self-Psychology and Spiritual Direction" in Robert J. Wicks, ed. *Handbook of Spirituality for Ministers* (Mahwah, N.J.: Paulist Press, 1995), 350–51. Gillespie offers numerous examples of this process, employing the psychological concepts applicable from self-psychology.

12. See Peter Rutter, *Sex in the Forbidden Zone* (Los Angeles: Jeremy Tarcher, 1989) for an illuminating discussion of this topic. See also Jane Becker and David Donovan, "Sexual Dynamics in Ministry Relationships" in *Human Development* 16 (Fall 1995): 23–27.

13. May, *Care of Mind/Care of Spirit*, 143–47.

14. See James O. Loughrun "Transference and Religious Practice," (*Journal of Pastoral Care* [September 1979]: 185–89) for the way even a "practice" can be the object of transference.

Epilogue

At the conclusion of *Spiritual Direction: Beyond the Beginnings*, it is only too apparent that I have addressed just a few of the advanced themes and issues facing spiritual directors. Each of us matures and hones our spiritual direction skills over time and in relationship to our own spiritual journey and the particular directees who gift us with their amazing journey into God. These interchanges with our directees frequently stimulate our reflection and stir our hearts. Sometimes these reflections and affections belong only to a particular directee, or God's Spirit uses them to nudge us personally into greater intimacy with God. At other times, when I notice that a cluster of directees begins to exhibit similar patterns and themes, I wonder if these insights belong to a larger audience. How many directors and their directees are traversing similar terrain without awareness of the others?

I am acutely aware that these reflections on some of the more mature dynamics of spiritual development and ways that directors can assist it represent only one strand of the mystical tradition. I have clearly emphasized throughout this volume the path of divine love as it manifests itself primarily in kataphatic ways. As discussed in chapter 4, this form of love mysticism engages images, affections, thoughts, and desires. Because our tradition has schooled us in wariness about this path, I am continually challenged to discern the truth of the caution and at the same time to rely on broad and consistent criteria for discernment in the tradition, which assesses not only the experiences and events that occur in prayer but also the entire quality and tenor of a person's life.

Our culture promotes the values of variety, change, and creativity over constancy, stability, and perseverance, and our lifetimes extend two to three times the length of our medieval predecessors. The process of mystical transformation can only transpire within the context of our actual lives. I have had the privilege of a number of long-term spiritual direction relationships with directees, and the interviews I have conducted as part of my research have opened a window onto the experience of the men and women with whom I spoke. Among those who persevered in season and out over twenty to thirty years of religious living will most likely recognize their experience in my descriptions. Some of the spiritual directors who recommended interviewees for my research sample were as convinced as I that the kinds of dynamics I describe in this volume—related to desire, resistance, intensifying intimacy with God, and movement through love mysticism into mutuality with God—are far more common than most people would think. Karl Rahner became convinced that this would be the case. He firmly held that the future of Christianity depended on this kind of mystical development.

While I have emphasized one variation on the spiritual journey in the context of this larger conversation on spiritual direction, I am equally aware of new experiences of God's absence endured by many people, who nevertheless continue to persevere in their spiritual practices and prayer forms. The profound dislocations and paradigm changes that characterize our postmodern era seem to set some of us on paths of fragmentation and darkness—experiences of God that emerge only against the background of loss, meaninglessness, and emptiness. Nevertheless, this path, whether persistent or transient in a given person's life, also arouses desire and finds fruition in some form of mutuality with God. Others have written about it more eloquently than I.

Although the directees who share their lives with me are affected by these cultural shifts and impasses, by and large they experience both intense forms of suffering and alienation in some aspects of their lives and God's simultaneous presence, luring them to recognize God's self-communication through beauty and loving intimacy.

"Beyond the beginnings" of spiritual direction and of the spiritual life almost anything can happen. I firmly believe that our task as spiritual directors requires us to continue to grow in skill and sensitivity in this ministry so that God's own Spirit might guide us and make us pliable and steady enough to serve all the ways God chooses to disclose and relate to us. As we accumulate, absorb, and encounter "new experiences" in our directees as well as in our own lives, we discover that we are both "beyond the beginnings" of becoming spiritual directors and, strangely, *always* beginning. May God never cease to amaze us and allure us.